READ WELL®

The Magic School Bus: Inside the Human Body

Teacher's Guide

Unit 20

Review

Note: See New and Important Objectives on page 2 for a complete list of skills taught and reviewed.

Critical Foundations in Primary Reading

Marilyn Sprick, Ann Watanabe, Karen Akiyama-Paik, and Shelley V. Jones

Sopris West®
EDUCATIONAL SERVICES

A Cambium Learning® Company

BOSTON, MA • LONGMONT, CO

ISBN 13-digit: 978-1-60218-543-2
ISBN 10-digit: 1-60218-543-3

7 8 9 10 11   B&B   16 15 14 13 12

167038/6-12

Table of Contents
Unit 20
The Magic School Bus: Inside the Human Body

Letter Sounds and Combinations

Cumulative Review of *Read Well 1* Sounds and Combinations (Ss, Ee, ee, Mm, Aa, Dd, th, Nn, Tt, Ww, Ii, Th, Hh, Cc, Rr, ea, sh, Sh, Kk, -ck, oo, ar, wh, Wh, ě, -y as in fly, Ll, Oo, Bb, all, Gg, Ff, Uu, er, oo as in book, Yy, a schwa, Pp, ay, Vv, Qq, Jj, Xx, or, Zz, a_e, -y as in baby, i_e, ou, ow as in cow, ch, Ch, ai, igh, o_e, ir) and:

Unit 2	Unit 3			Unit 5	Unit 6
aw	**ew**	**ue**	**u_e**	**ow**	**ge**
/aw/	/o͞o/	/o͞o/	/o͞o/	/ō͞o/	/j/
Paw	**Crew**	**Blue**	**Flute**	**Snow**	**Page**
Voiced	Voiced	Voiced	Bossy E Voiced	Voiced (Long)	Voiced

Unit 6	Unit 7		Unit 8		Unit 10
-dge	**ci**	**ce**	**kn**	**ph**	**oa**
/j/	/sss/	/sss/	/nnn/	/fff/	/ō͞o/
Badge	**Circle**	**Center**	**Knee**	**Phone**	**Boat**
Voiced	Unvoiced	Unvoiced	Voiced	Unvoiced	Voiced (Long)

Unit 11		Unit 12		Unit 13
oi	**ea**	**gi**	**au**	**oy**
/oi/	/ĕĕĕ/	/j/	/au/	/oy/
Point	**Bread**	**Giraffe**	**Astronaut**	**Boy**
Voiced	Voiced (Short)	Voiced	Voiced	Voiced

Affixes (including morphographs—affixes taught with meaning) and Open Syllables

Cumulative Review of *Read Well 1* Affixes (-ed, -en, -es, -ing, -ly, -s, -y, -tion) and:

Unit 2	Unit 3		Unit 5		Unit 6
re-	**un-**	**ex-**	**o**	**-ful**	**bi-**
Means again	**Means not**		Open syllable /ō/	**Means full of**	**Means two**
as in reread	as in unhappy	as in excited	as in open and moment	as in colorful	as in bicycle

Unit 7	Unit 8	Unit 11	Unit 12	Unit 13	
de-	**-able**	**i**	**be-**	**-ous**	**dis-**
		Open syllable /ī/			
as in detective	as in comfortable	as in silence and pilot	as in before	as in enormous	as in discover

Unit 14		Unit 15		Unit 16	
-al	**-ible**	**-or**	**-ment**	**-ic**	**pre-**
		Means one who			**Means before**
as in animal	as in flexible	as in actor	as in apartment	as in scientific	as in preview

Unit 17		Unit 18		Unit 19	
-ity	**-sion**	**-ness**	**-less**	**in-**	**im-**
			Means without		**Means not**
as in activity	as in permission	as in fairness	as in helpless	as in insert	as in impossible

Introduction
Magic School Bus

Story Notes

The Magic School Bus: Inside the Human Body—Ride along with Ms. Frizzle and her students as the Magic School Bus makes its way through the human body. Your students will learn all kinds of fascinating facts: What is the body made of? What is the tube that leads from the mouth to the stomach? What is the purpose of the small intestine? These and other scientific facts are presented to students in fun, easy-to-grasp, and humorous ways. We hope this introduction to Ms. Frizzle will get your kids hooked on science and the Magic School Bus series.

Recommended Read Alouds

The *Read Well 2* suggested Read Alouds enhance small group instruction—providing opportunities to further build background knowledge and vocabulary.

A Drop of Blood by Paul Showers
Nonfiction • Science
Blood is everywhere in your body—your fingers and toes, your arms and legs, sometimes dripping down your nose. What is blood made of, and what does it do? Find out more about a vampire's favorite snack.

Germs Make Me Sick by Melvin Berger
Nonfiction • Science
"Everyone knows that germs can make you sick. But not everyone knows how." So opens Melvin Berger's book about germs. Students learn what germs look like, how they interact with the body, and the difference between bacteria and viruses.

Read Well Connections
In this unit, students build knowledge of how the body works. Both Read Alouds add to the facts presented in the Magic School Bus book.

> **CAUTION
> (Reminder)**
> Do not read the Read Aloud recommendations during small group instruction. Reserve this time for students to read.

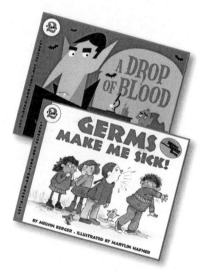

NOTE FROM THE AUTHORS

ICING ON THE CAKE

With Unit 20, your students will demonstrate how sophisticated their reading has become. They will take command of content words such as "esophagus," "cerebellum," and "circulate." They will be able to explain awesome facts about human anatomy. Parents, peers, and other teachers will be amazed as your students explain why white blood cells are important. This unit may be a springboard to further research and inquiry.

With Unit 20, your second grade students are well on their way to reading significantly above grade level. Students who continued their second grade year with *Read Well 2 Plus* (Units 21–25) scored an average grade equivalency of 3.82 on the Woodcock Reading Mastery Short Scale, Total Reading (Word Identification and Passage Comprehension).

Knowledge is indeed power.

New and Important Objectives
A Research-Based Reading Program

Phonemic Awareness
Phonics
Fluency
Vocabulary
Comprehension

Phonics

Cumulative Letter Sounds and Combinations

Review • Ss, Ee, ee, Mm, Aa, Dd, th, Nn, Tt, Ww, Ii, Th, Hh, Cc, Rr, ea, sh, Sh, Kk, -ck, oo, ar, wh, Wh, ĕ, -y (as in fly), Ll, Oo, Bb, all, Gg, Ff, Uu, er, oo (as in book), Yy, a (schwa), Pp, ay, Vv, Qq, Jj, Xx, or, Zz, a_e, -y (as in baby), i_e, ou, ow (as in cow), ch, Ch, ai, igh, o_e, ir, aw, ew, ue, u_e, ow (as in snow), ge, -dge, ci, ce, kn, ph, oa, oi, ea (as in bread), gi, au, oy

Cumulative Affixes, Morphographs, and Open Syllables

Review • -ed, -en, -er, -es, -est, -ing, -ly, -s, -y, -tion, re-, un-, ex-, o (as in open), -ful, bi-, de-, -able, i (as in silence), be-, dis-, -ous, -al, -ible, -or, -ment, -ic, pre-, -ity, -sion, -ness, -less, in-, im-

★New Proper Nouns

Alex, Amanda, Arnold, Arnold's ◆ Carmen, Cheesie-Weesies, Dorothy, Florrie, Friz, Gregory, Ms. Frizzle, Ms. Frizzle's, Phil, Phoebe, Shirley, Wanda

★New Contractions

when's

★New Pattern Words

bile ◆ blob ◆ buds ◆ choo, churning, churns, cord ◆ dull, force, germ, germs, glimpse ◆ gross, grossed, ick, key, nerve, nerves, ode, ooh, sac, scrape, slight, sour ◆ stem ◆ stir ◆ thud

*Known Pattern Words With Affixes • badly, beats, bleeding, branched, chasing, coiled, ending, fats, floated, flowed, gases, goodness, kinder, landing, mashing, passing, pinkish, pounding, pumps, refresh, regrow, roundness, safer, seated, smarter, sooner, strangest, stretching, tests, turning

★New Compound and Hyphenated Words

bloodstream, built-in, daydream, daydreaming ◆ filmstrip ◆ front-runner, gallbladder ◆ hamburger, heartbeat, otherwise, pipelines ◆ toothpaste ◆ toothpick, windpipe

---

* Known Pattern Words With Affixes, Known Tricky Words With Affixes, and **Known Multisyllabic Words With Affixes** have base words students have previously read. The words are new in this unit because they have not been previously read with the affix.

★ = New in this unit

◆ = Words that are not introduced in the exercises before they are read in the storybook

Phonics (continued)

★ Other New Multisyllabic Words

actions, anatomy, announced, arranged, author, behave, bladder, carbon dioxide, cavity, cerebellum, cerebral, circulate, circulates, circulating, circulation, constantly, contract ◆ correct, cortex, deafening, delivery, disease, emerge, emerged, enlarged, enter, equal, esophagus ◆ fatty, fiber ◆ flavors, fluid, fluids, function, functions, gurgle, gurgling, hankie, ignition, intestine, intestines, iodine, kidneys, liver, meters, microscope, molecules, nasal, ok, organ, organs, outer, oxygen, pasta, plasma, platelets, prepare, processor, products, recess, relief, saucer, saucers, solar, solution, spinal ◆ supply, terrific, tremendous, urine, vessel, vessels, video, villi, vitamins ◆ wrinkled, yogurt

*Known Multisyllabic Words With Affixes • body's, bottomless, bundles, circles, controlled, controls, destroying, destroys, detecting, digested, digestion, digestive, disgusting, museums, poisons, stretchable, tickles, tickling, yellowish

★ New Tricky Words

bacteria, cereal, gesundheit, poultry, pressure, receiving, system, tissues, tour, wanna

*Known Tricky Words With Affixes • answers, educational, greatly, pieces, worrying

Fluency

Accuracy, Expression, Phrasing, Rate

Vocabulary

New • anatomy, break down, circulate, circulation, constantly, control, daydream, emerge, esophagus, exhibit, experiment, fluid, function, glimpse, liquid, organ, oxygen, relief, unless, upset, waste

Review • absurd, adventure, amazing, classify, connect, destroy, digest, distressed, energy, fascinate, food chain, frantic, panic, popular, senses, trade

Reviewed in Context • absolutely, amazed, amazing, caption, carnivore, connect, destroy, digest, disgusting, energy, except, exhausted, herbivore, imaginative, impossible, panic, pant, protect, realize, recognized, recycle, senses, surface, trade, wonderful

Idioms and Expressions

New • business as usual, get rid of, have a heart, lose my nerve, swept out

Review • false alarm, going too far

Comprehension

Unit Genres

Fiction • With Factual Content

Comprehension Processes

Build Knowledge: Factual, Procedural, Conceptual

Day	1	2	3	4	5	6
Remember						
Defining						
Identifying (recalling)	S,C	S,C	S,C	S	C	C
Using						
Understand						
Defining (in your own words)	S	S	S,C	S,C		S,C
Describing				S	S	S
Explaining (rephrasing)	S	S,C	S,C	S	S	S
Illustrating	C			C		
Sequencing			C			
Summarizing	S,C	S	S,C		S	S
Using	S,C	S	S,C	S,C	S,C	S,C
Visualizing	C			C		
Apply						
Demonstrating						
Explaining (unstated)	S,C	S,C	S	S	S,C	S,C
Illustrating		C				
Inferring	S	S,C	S	S	S	S,C
Making Connections (relating)	S					
Predicting	S		S	S		S
Using	S	S	S	S	S	S
Analyze						
Classifying						
Comparing/Contrasting						
Distinguishing Cause/Effect				S	S	
Drawing Conclusions						C
Inferring					S	
Evaluate						
Making Judgments						
Responding (personal)				S		S
Create						
Generating Ideas	C					

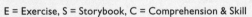

E = Exercise, S = Storybook, C = Comprehension & Skill

Comprehension (continued)

Skills and Strategies

Day	1	2	3	4	5	6
Priming Background Knowledge						
Setting a Purpose for Reading		S	S		S	
Answering Questions	S	S	S	S	S	
Asking Questions						
Visualizing						
Comprehension Monitoring/Fix Ups						
Does it Make Sense?	C	C	C		C	
Looking Back						
Restating						
Summarizing						
Main Idea	C					
Retelling						
Supporting Details	C		C			
Understanding Text Structure						
Title, Author, Illustrator	S,C					
Fact or Fiction	S					
Genre (Classifying)						
Narrative						
Setting	S					
Main Character/Traits (Characterization)						
Goal						
Problem/Solution						
Action/Events/Sequence		S,C				
Outcome/Conclusion						
Lesson/Author's Message						
Expository						
Subject/Topic						C
Heading						
Supporting Details (Facts/Information)	S,C	S,C	S	S,C	S,C	C
Main Idea			C	S		C
Using Graphic Organizers						
Chart						
Diagram (labeling)		C	C	C	C	
Hierarchy (topic/detail)	C					C
K-W-L						
Map (locating, labeling)						
Matrix (compare/contrast)						
Sequence (linear, cycle, cause and effect)			C		C	
Story Map						
Web						

E = Exercise, S = Storybook, C = Comprehension & Skill

Comprehension (continued)

Study Skills

Day	1	2	3	4	5	6
Alphabetical Order				C		
Following Directions						
Locating Information	C	C	S,C	S		
Note Taking						
Previewing						
Reviewing		S		S	S	S
Test Taking		C				C
Using Glossary						
Using Table of Contents						
Viewing	S,C	C	S,C	S,C	S,C	S
Verifying						

Writing in Response to Reading

Day	1	2	3	4	5	6
Sentence Completion	C	C	C	C	C	
Making Lists						
Sentence Writing	C	C	C	C		C
Story Retell/Summary						
Fact Summary	C					
Paragraph Writing	C					C
Report Writing						
Open-Ended Response						
Creative Writing						

Writing Traits

(Addressed within the context of Writing in Response to Reading)

Day	1	2	3	4	5	6
Ideas and Content						
Elaborating/Generating						C
Organization						
Introduction						
Topic Sentence	C					
Supporting Details	C					
Sequencing						
Word Choice						
Sophisticated Words (Tier 2 and 3)	C					
Conventions						
Capital	C	C		C	C	C
Ending Punctuation	C	C	C	C	C	C
Other (commas, quotation marks)						
Presentation						
Handwriting	C			C		C
Neatness	C			C		C

E = Exercise, S = Storybook, C = Comprehension & Skill

Daily Lesson Planning

LESSON PLAN FORMAT

Teacher-Directed 45 Minutes		Independent Teacher-Directed, as needed
Lesson Part 1 (Phonological Awareness, Phonics, Fluency, Comprehension) 15–20 Minutes	**Lesson Part 2** (Vocabulary, Fluency, Comprehension) 20–25 Minutes	**Lesson Part 3** (Vocabulary, Fluency, Comprehension) 15–20 Minutes

• Exercises	• Unit and/or Story Opener
	
	• Vocabulary
	
	• Interactive Story Reading
	
	• Short Passage Practice
	  Timed Readings
		• Story Reading With Partner
		  or Whisper Reading
		
		• Comprehension and Skill
		  Activities

HOMEWORK

Read Well Homework (blackline masters of new *Read Well 2* passages) provides an opportunity for children to celebrate accomplishments with parents. Homework should be sent home on routine days.

ORAL READING FLUENCY ASSESSMENT

Upon completion of this unit, assess each student and proceed to Unit 21, as appropriate.

WRITTEN ASSESSMENT

During the time students would normally complete Comprehension and Skill Activities, students will be administered a Written Assessment that can be found on page 127 in the students' *Activity Book 3*.

Note: See Making Decisions for additional assessment information.

DIFFERENTIATED LESSON PLANS

The differentiated lesson plans illustrate how to use materials for students with various learning needs. As you set up your unit plan, always include *Read Well 2* Exercises and Story Reading on a daily basis. Unit 20 includes 6- and 8-Day Plans.

Plans	For groups that:
6-DAY	Complete Oral Reading Fluency Assessments with Passes and Strong Passes
8-DAY	Complete Oral Reading Fluency Assessments with Passes and require teacher-guided assistance with Story Reading and Comprehension and Skill Work

6-DAY PLAN

Day 1

Teacher-Directed
• Exercise 1
• Story Opener: The Magic School Bus: Inside the Human Body
• Vocabulary
• Inside the Human Body, pages 4–7
• Guide practice, as needed, on Comp & Skill 1, 2

Independent Work
• Repeated Reading: Partner or Whisper Read, Inside the Human Body, pages 4–7
• Comp & Skill 1, 2

Homework
• Homework Passage 1

Day 2

Teacher-Directed
• Exercise 2
• Vocabulary
• Inside the Human Body, pages 8–11
• Guide practice, as needed, on Comp & Skill 3, Human Body Cover and Entry 1

Independent Work
• On Your Own: Partner or Whisper Read, Inside the Human Body, pages 12 and 13
• Comp & Skill 3, Human Body Cover and Entry 1

Homework
• Homework Passage 2

Day 3

Teacher-Directed
• Exercise 3
• Vocabulary
• Inside the Human Body, pages 14–17
• Guide practice, as needed, on Comp & Skill 4, Human Body Entry 2

Independent Work
• On Your Own: Partner or Whisper Read, Inside the Human Body, pages 18 and 19
• Comp & Skill 4, Human Body Entry 2

Homework
• Homework Passage 3

Day 4

Teacher-Directed
• Exercise 4
• Vocabulary
• Inside the Human Body, pages 20–23
• Guide practice, as needed, on Extra Fluency Passage (optional), Comp & Skill 5, Human Body Entry 3

Independent Work
• Repeated Reading: Partner or Whisper Read, Inside the Human Body, pages 20–23
• Comp & Skill 5, Human Body Entry 3, Extra Fluency Passage (optional)

Homework
• Homework Passage 4

Day 5

Teacher-Directed
• Exercise 5
• Vocabulary
• Inside the Human Body, pages 24–27
• Guide practice, as needed, on Comp & Skill 6, Human Body Entry 4

Independent Work
• On Your Own: Partner or Whisper Read, Inside the Human Body, pages 28–31
• Comp & Skill 6, Human Body Entry 4

Homework
• Homework Passage 5

Day 6

Teacher-Directed
• Exercise 6
• Vocabulary
• Inside the Human Body, pages 32–37

Independent Work
• Written Assessment
• Oral Reading Fluency Assessment*

Homework
• Homework Passage 6

Note: Unit 20 features an extra Fluency Passage, located before Comp & Skill Activity 5, and a Just for Fun Comp & Skill Activity, located after Comp & Skill Activity 6. Just for Fun can be used as part of Day 5 activities or anytime after students read page 32.

* The Oral Reading Fluency Assessments are individually administered by the teacher while students are working on their Written Assessments.

Day 1

Teacher-Directed
- Exercise 1
- Story Opener: The Magic School Bus: Inside the Human Body
- Vocabulary
- Inside the Human Body, pages 4–7
- Guide practice, as needed, on Comp & Skill 1, 2

Independent Work
- Repeated Reading: Partner or Whisper Read, Inside the Human Body, pages 4–7
- Comp & Skill 1, 2

Homework
- Homework Passage 1

Day 2

Teacher-Directed
- Exercise 2
- Vocabulary
- Inside the Human Body, pages 8–11
- Guide practice, as needed, on Comp & Skill 3, Human Body Cover and Entry 1

Independent Work
- On Your Own: Partner or Whisper Read, Inside the Human Body, pages 12–13
- Comp & Skill 3, Human Body Cover and Entry 1

Homework
- Homework Passage 2

Day 3

Teacher-Directed
- Exercise 3
- Vocabulary
- Inside the Human Body, pages 14–17
- Guide practice, as needed, on Comp & Skill 4, Human Body Entry 2

Independent Work
- Repeated Reading: Partner or Whisper Read, Inside the Human Body, pages 14–17
- Comp & Skill 4, Human Body Entry 2

Homework
- Homework Passage 3

Day 4

Teacher-Directed
- Review Exercise 3
- Vocabulary
- Inside the Human Body, pages 18–19
- Guide practice, as needed, on Comp & Skill 5, Extra Fluency Passage

Independent Work
- Repeated Reading: Partner or Whisper Read, Inside the Human Body, pages 18–19
- Comp & Skill 5, Extra Fluency Passage

Homework
- Fluency Passage

Day 5

Teacher-Directed
- Exercise 4
- Review Vocabulary
- Inside the Human Body, pages 20–23
- Guide practice, as needed, on Human Body Entry 3

Independent Work
- Repeated Reading: Partner or Whisper Read, Inside the Human Body, pages 20–23
- Human Body Entry 3

Homework
- Homework Passage 4

Day 6

Teacher-Directed
- Exercise 5
- Vocabulary
- Inside the Human Body, pages 24–27
- Guide practice, as needed, on Human Body Entry 4

Independent Work
- Repeated Reading: Partner or Whisper Read, Inside the Human Body, pages 24–27
- Human Body Entry 4

Homework
- Homework Passage 5

Day 7

Teacher-Directed
- Review Exercise 5
- Review Vocabulary
- Inside the Human Body, pages 28–31
- Guide practice, as needed, on Comp & Skill 6, Just for Fun (optional)

Independent Work
- Repeated Reading: Partner or Whisper Read, Inside the Human Body, pages 28–31
- Comp & Skill 6, Just for Fun (optional)

Homework
- Teacher's Choice

Day 8

Teacher-Directed
- Exercise 6
- Vocabulary
- Inside the Human Body, pages 32–37

Independent Work
- Written Assessment
- Oral Reading Fluency Assessment*

Homework
- Homework Passage 6

Materials and Materials Preparation

Core Lessons

Teacher Materials

READ WELL 2 MATERIALS

- Unit 20 Teacher's Guide
- Sound Cards
- Unit 20 Oral Reading Fluency Assessment found on page 104
- Group Assessment Record found in the *Assessment Manual*

SCHOOL SUPPLIES

Stopwatch or watch with a second hand

Student Materials

READ WELL 2 MATERIALS (for each student)

- *Magic School Bus: Inside the Human Body*
- *Exercise Book 3*
- *Activity Book 3* or copies of Unit 20 Comprehension and Skill Work
- Unit 20 Written Assessment found in *Activity Book 3*, page 127, and on the blackline master CD.
- Unit 20 Certificate of Achievement (blackline master page 105)
- Unit 20 Homework (blackline masters)
  See *Getting Started* for suggested homework routines.

SCHOOL SUPPLIES

Pencils, colors (optional—markers, crayons, or colored pencils)

Make one copy per student of each blackline master, as appropriate for the group.

Note: For new or difficult Comprehension and Skill Activities, make overhead transparencies from the blackline masters. Use the transparencies to demonstrate and guide practice.

SPECIAL NOTE

Your students will complete a human body folder. For ease of use, pull pages 89–92 out of *Activity Book 3*. Tape the pages down the center to create a folder.

Acknowledging Accomplishments
Multisyllabic Word Fluency

Acknowledging Accomplishments

As you approach the end of the school year, keep your students motivated. Use words, privileges, personal records, and notes to keep the kids excited about their ongoing accomplishments.

CELEBRATE ACCOMPLISHMENTS—WHETHER BIG OR SMALL

When students meet your expectations, acknowledge individuals and provide descriptive feedback.

[Joshua] and [Ellen], nice job with your extra Partner Reading. You both increased your fluency on this unit. Super job!

Provide attention with privileges.

• [Natasha], you brought your homework back two days this week. I'm very proud of you. You get to be Homework Checker.

• [Tyrell], you waited for your turn, so you get to call on people to read.

Use physical demonstrations.

Everyone, air clap for [Kate]. She just beat her personal best!

Write notes home that congratulate students and family members. Acknowledgements are motivating.

• Write notes to family members thanking them for their participation.

• Give kids sticky notes to acknowledge their accomplishments.

  [Angie], you get a sticky note with the word *circulate*. You used that snazzy word in your answer. Good thinking.

Have students keep records of their personal best.

• Provide each student with a Personal Best Scrapbook.
  At the end of each unit, have students review their work and add their favorite written work to the scrapbook.

• Place each child's personal best oral reading fluency score on a sticky note in his or her reading folder. Replace, with fanfare, as appropriate.

SAMPLE PARENT NOTE

Dear Mrs. Cowley,

Jan brought her homework back to school every day this week.

You can be very proud of the responsibility she has shown.

Thank you for your assistance.

Sincerely,
Mrs. Bird

---

circulate

Multisyllabic Word Reading Fluency

As good readers do, your students will continue to read big words from left to right, chunking common letter patterns. Then students will use their English oral language skills to pronounce the words they know.

ACCURACY FIRST

Follow the procedures for teaching the Decoding Exercises to ensure that students are accurate at reading multisyllabic words before working on fluency.

- Have students read the words by parts.
- Have students read the whole word.
- Gently correct errors and have students reread.
- Return to difficult words for three correct responses.
- Reread the column or row until students are 100% accurate.
- Reread, mixing group and individual turns, to build fluency.

> "Many big words occur infrequently, but when they do occur, they carry much of the meaning and content of what is being read . . . (Cunningham, 1998, p 189).

FLUENCY PRACTICE SUGGESTIONS

Once students are accurate, have students practice reading lists for fluency.

Have students chorally read the column.

Say something like:

Let's practice for fluency.

Set a pace. Read about this fast: emerged, contract, nasal, functions, fiber . . .

Your turn. (emerged, contract, nasal . . .)

Now read each word two times. Let the words roll off your tongue.

(emerged, emerged; contract, contract . . .)

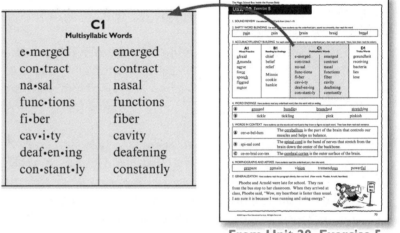

From Unit 20, Exercise 5

DURING STORY READING

Remind students to use their part-by-part strategy. Say something like:

If you see a big word that is difficult, remember to use your strategy for reading big words. Get the word started by saying the parts. Don't stop.

During Story Reading, if a student stalls, don't wait. Gently start the part-by-part reading. If the sentence is "Different parts of the mouth have taste buds that are best at detecting different flavors," your assistance might be as follows:

(Different parts of the mouth have taste buds that are best at . . .) **de-tect** . . . (detecting different flavors.)

In this example, you help with just the first and/or second syllable. After the Story Reading, put any difficult words on the board and have students practice for accuracy and fluency. For additional practice, you may wish to periodically write a new sentence on the board with the difficult word.

How to Teach the Lessons

Teach from this section. Each instructional component is outlined in an easy-to-teach format.

Exercise 1

- Story Opener: The Magic School Bus: Inside the Human Body
- Vocabulary
- Story Reading 1
  With the Teacher: Pages 4–7
- Comprehension and Skill Activities 1, 2

Exercise 2

- Vocabulary
- Story Reading 2
  With the Teacher: Pages 8–11
  On Your Own: Pages 12 and 13
- Comprehension and Skill Activity 3, Human Body Cover and Entry 1

Exercise 3

- Vocabulary
- Story Reading 3
  With the Teacher: Pages 14–17
  On Your Own: Pages 18 and 19
- Comprehension and Skill Activity 4, Human Body Entry 2

Exercise 4

- Vocabulary
- Story Reading 4
  With the Teacher: Pages 20–23
  Extra Fluency Passage (optional)
- Comprehension and Skill Activity 5, Human Body Entry 3

Exercise 5

- Story Reading 5
  With the Teacher: Pages 24–27
  On Your Own: Pages 28–31
- Comprehension and Skill Activity 6, Human Body Entry 4

Exercise 6

- Vocabulary
- Story Reading 6
  With the Teacher: Pages 32–37
- Written Assessment

Note: Lessons include daily homework.

1 **SOUND REVIEW**

2 **SOUND PRACTICE**

PACING

Exercise 1 should take about 15 minutes.

- For each task, have students spell and say the focus sound in the gray bar. For Bossy E and Rhyming Words, read the header.
- Next, have students read each underlined sound, the word, then the whole column.
- Repeat with each column, building accuracy first, then fluency.

3 **ACCURACY AND FLUENCY BUILDING**

- For each task, have students say any underlined part, then read the word.
- Set a pace. Then have students read the whole words in each task and column.
- Provide repeated practice, building accuracy first, then fluency.

C1. Rhyming Words

Have students read the words and identify what's the same about them.

D1. Contractions

For each set of words, have students read the words, then the contraction.

E1. Tricky Words

- For each Tricky Word, have students use the sounds and word parts they know to silently sound out the word. Use the word in a sentence to help with pronunciation.

pressure
Look at the first word. You already know part of this word. Read the small word. (sure) Now read the whole word. (pressure) The soccer game was tied with one minute left. The players felt a lot of . . . *pressure*. Read the word two times. (pressure, pressure)

trouble	When our dog chewed on the couch, he got into . . . *trouble*.
pieces	Miranda cut the straw into several short . . . *pieces*.
actually	We have been friends for years. We have . . . *actually* . . . been friends for ten years.
weird	Some sea creatures look very strange, or . . . *weird*.

- Have students go back and read the whole words in the column.

4 **MULTISYLLABIC WORDS**

For each word, have students read the syllables, then the whole word. Use the word in a sentence, as appropriate.

announced	"The storm is over," the weatherman . . . *announced*.
iodine	Pablo's mom treated his scraped knee with a medicine called . . . *iodine*.
microscope	In science class, we can see really, really tiny things with a . . . *microscope*.
solution	We mixed bleach and water to make a cleaning . . . *solution*.
anatomy	The science teacher used a skeleton to teach the class about . . . *anatomy*.
museum	I would like to go on a field trip to a . . . *museum*.

5 **MORPHOGRAPHS AND AFFIXES**

- Have students read the underlined part, then the word.
- Review the meaning of the morphograph *re-*, as time allows.
- Repeat practice with whole words, mixing group and individual turns. Build accuracy, then fluency.

6 GENERALIZATION: READING NEW WORDS IN PARAGRAPHS
- Have students read the paragraph silently, then out loud. Tell students to use the sounds and word parts they know to read any difficult words.
- Repeat practice, as needed.

The Magic School Bus: Inside the Human Body

Unit 20 Exercise 1
Use before pages 4–7

1. SOUND REVIEW Have students review sounds for accuracy, then for fluency.

A	oy	ew	gi	oi	-dge
B	au	oa	u_e	ce	aw

2. SOUND PRACTICE In each column, have students spell and say the sound, next say any underlined sound and the word, then read the column.

ce, ci	-y as in baby	ge as in page	Bossy E	Rhyming Words
cell	jelly	strangest	scrape	carnivore
decided	body	gently	slide	omnivore
science	tiny	change	inside	herbivore

3. ACCURACY/FLUENCY BUILDING For each column, have students say any underlined part, then read each word. Next, have them read the column.

A1 Mixed Practice	B1 Names	C1 Rhyming Words	D1 Contractions	E1 Tricky Words
cheek	Rachel	millions	when is	pressure
magic	Ms. Frizzle	billions	when's	trouble
jail	Gregory	trillions		pieces
know			we are	actually
ode			we're	weird

4. MULTISYLLABIC WORDS Have students read each word part, then read each whole word.

A	an·nounced	announced	i·o·dine	iodine
B	mi·cro·scope	microscope	so·lu·tion	solution
C	a·na·to·my	anatomy	mu·se·um	museum

5. MORPHOGRAPHS AND AFFIXES Have students read the underlined part, then the word.

experiment	beginning	exhibit	regrow

6. GENERALIZATION Have students read the paragraph silently, then out loud. (New words: Arnold, recess, ooh)

Cass and her friend Arnold decided to stay in class during recess to write a poem. Cass was excited because she liked to write, but it wasn't Arnold's favorite thing to do. Arnold groaned, "Ooh, I don't have energy for this. I'd rather be out playing."

65

Have students tell you the team expectations. Say something like: Who can tell me the first two team rules?
1. Sit up.
2. Follow directions.
3. Help each other.
4. Work hard and have fun.

ACKNOWLEDGE STUDENTS WHEN THEY MEET YOUR EXPECTATIONS (Reminder)

Students respond positively when you acknowledge their accomplishments. Pair descriptive praise with an individual turn or job. [Allie], great job sitting up and finger tracking. Everyone, watch how [Allie] is able to follow along while I read.

GENERALIZATION (Reminder)

The generalization task provides an opportunity for you to informally assess students' ability to read new words that have not been pretaught.

15

COMPREHENSION PROCESSES
Remember, Apply

PROCEDURES

1. Introducing the Storybook

Identifying—Title
Have students identify the title of their new storybook.
Say something like:
Everyone, look at the cover of the book.
What's the title of this book?
(The Magic School Bus: Inside the Human Body)

2. Introducing the Title Page

Identifying—Author, Illustrator; Making Connections; Using Vocabulary— popular; Viewing; Inferring
Now turn to the title page.
The title page will tell you who wrote the book and who illustrated it.
Who is the author? (Joanna Cole)
Who is the illustrator? (Bruce Degen)

Joanna Cole and Bruce Degen have teamed up to write and illustrate a whole series of Magic School Bus books.

Raise your hand if you've read some of these books.

Everyone, take a minute and look through the pages. See if you can figure out why the books are *popular*.
(I think kids like the books because they have fun illustrations. They are about kids. They are about interesting topics. It's kind of like a comic book. The kids talk . . .)

I like these books because even though they're very imaginative, they also have a lot of real science information in them. Every time I read a Magic School Bus book, I learn something new.

The Magic School Bus
Inside the Human Body

By Joanna Cole / Illustrated by Bruce Degen

Scholastic Inc.
New York · Toronto · London · Auckland · Sydney
Mexico City · New Delhi · Hong Kong · Buenos Aires

COMPREHENSION PROCESSES

Understand, Apply

PROCEDURES

1. Introducing Vocabulary

★ **experiment** ★ **anatomy, energy**

- For each vocabulary word, have students read the word by parts, then read the whole word.
- Read the student-friendly explanations to students as they follow with their fingers. Then have students use the vocabulary word by following the gray text.
- Review and discuss the illustrations.
  Note: Student vocabulary pages for this unit are found in the students' *Exercise Book 3*.

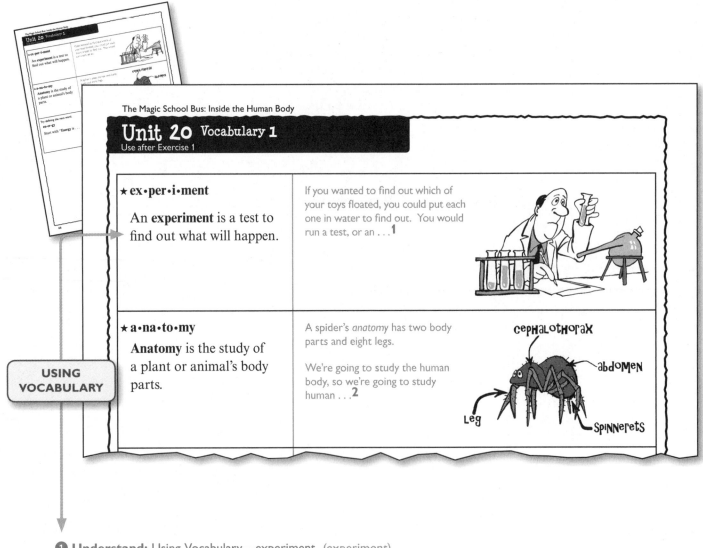

The Magic School Bus: Inside the Human Body

Unit 20 Vocabulary 1
Use after Exercise 1

USING VOCABULARY

★ **ex·per·i·ment**

An **experiment** is a test to find out what will happen.

If you wanted to find out which of your toys floated, you could put each one in water to find out. You would run a test, or an . . . **1**

★ **a·na·to·my**

Anatomy is the study of a plant or animal's body parts.

A spider's *anatomy* has two body parts and eight legs.

We're going to study the human body, so we're going to study human . . . **2**

cephalothorax

abdomen

leg

spinnerets

1 Understand: Using Vocabulary—experiment (experiment)

2 Apply: Using Vocabulary—anatomy (anatomy)

★ = New in this unit

2. Now You Try It!
- Have students read the last word by parts and then read the whole word.
- Have students explain or define the word in their own words, then use the word in a sentence.

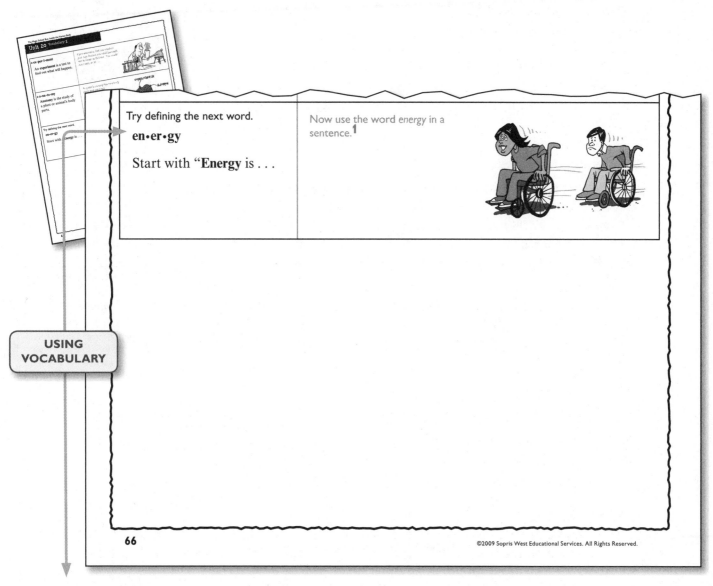

Try defining the next word.

en•er•gy

Start with "**Energy** is . . .

Now use the word *energy* in a sentence.[1]

66

USING VOCABULARY

❶ **Understand:** Defining and Using Vocabulary—energy (Energy is the power to do things. Eating healthy food gives me energy.)

STORY READING INSTRUCTIONS

Students read pages 4–7 with the teacher.

COMPREHENSION PROCESSES

Remember, Understand, Apply

COMPREHENSION BUILDING

If students have difficulty comprehending, think aloud with them or reread the portion of the story that answers the question. Repeat the question.

PROCEDURES

1. **Introducing pages 4–7**

    Viewing; Identifying—Setting, What; Inferring; Explaining; Predicting
    Discuss the page set-up and pictures. Say something like:

    Turn to page 4. This book is a lot of fun. Part of it is like a comic book. The characters think and talk in speech balloons and thought bubbles. Find what the boy in the yellow and white T-shirt is thinking. What is he thinking? (I can't take the pressure.)

    Where does this part of the story take place? (It takes place in a classroom.)
    That's right. The book also has a lot of student work in it. Touch the posters on the wall.
    As we read the book, we'll learn a lot of interesting information from the kids' work.

    What is Ms. Frizzle doing? (She is teaching the class. She's explaining something . . .)
    Look at the kids. How do they look? Do they look excited, happy, bored?
    (Some look bored. Some look worried. Some are goofing off or talking . . .)
    [Some of you know about Ms. Frizzle.] What do you think is going to happen?
    (The kids are going to go on a trip inside a human body.)

    > **CORRECTING DECODING ERRORS**
    > During story reading, gently correct any error, then have students reread the sentence.

2. **First Reading**
    *   Ask questions and discuss the story as indicated by the blue text in this guide.
    *   Mix group and individual turns, independent of your voice.
        Have students work toward a group accuracy goal of 0–4 errors.
    *   After reading the story, practice any difficult words. Reread as needed.

3. **Second Reading, Short Passage Practice: Developing Prosody**
    *   Demonstrate expressive, fluent reading of the first paragraph.
        Read at a rate slightly faster than the students' rate.
    *   Guide practice with your voice.
    *   Provide individual turns while others track with their fingers and whisper read.
    *   Repeat with the speech balloons and thought bubbles.

4. **Partner or Whisper Reading: Repeated Reading**
     Before beginning independent work, have students finger track and partner or whisper read.

5. Comprehension and Skill Work

For students on a 6-Day Plan, tell them they will do Comprehension and Skill Activities 1 and 2 after they read on their own. Guide practice, as needed. For teacher directions, see pages 25 and 26. (For an 8-Day Plan, see the Lesson Planner, page 9.)

6. Homework 1: New Passage

After Reading Page 4

❶ Remember: Identifying—How
How did the kids know trouble was about to start?
(The kids said they knew there would be trouble because Ms. Frizzle is the strangest teacher in the school.)

❷ Apply: Inferring, Explaining
What does Arnold mean by "I can't take the pressure!"?
(He means that he's not happy. Ms. Frizzle said that Arnold should be interested.)

❸ Apply: Viewing; Inferring; Using Vocabulary—food chain, classify
Look at the posters on the wall. What do you think the class has been studying?
(The class has been studying classifying animals . . . They've probably been studying food chains.)

After Reading Page 5

❶ **Apply:** Inferring, Explaining
I'm not sure the kids are excited about studying the human body. What do you think? Why?
(They aren't happy about it. They look bored. They're saying things like "When's recess?")

After Reading Page 6

❶ **Remember:** Identifying—Fact
Rachel wrote a fact sheet about cells. What did she tell you about your body?
(It's made of trillions of cells.)

❷ **Understand:** Explaining; Using Vocabulary—experiment
Ms. Frizzle had the students do an experiment. What was the experiment?
(The experiment was to take cells from inside your mouth and look at them under a microscope.)

After Reading Page 7

❶ Understand: Summarizing—Facts
Gregory's fact sheet identified three different jobs that cells in your body do.
What are those jobs?
(Lung cells help you breathe, muscle cells help you move, and brain cells help you think.)

❷ Remember: Identifying—Where
Where is the class going?
(They are going to a science museum.)

❸ Apply: Using Vocabulary—exhibit; Inferring
Museums collect special things that you can see, study, and learn about. These collections are called
exhibits. Some museums have dinosaur exhibits. Others have African exhibits, and others have exhibits
about American history. There are many kinds of exhibits in museums. What kind of exhibit do you think
Ms. Frizzle's class is going to see?
(They are going to see a human body exhibit.)

❹ Apply: Inferring; Explaining; Using Vocabulary—distressed, energy
Do you think Arnold is excited about the class trip? How can you tell?
(No. He looks worried, unhappy, distressed. He thinks being in Ms. Frizzle's class takes all his energy . . .)

STORY COMPREHENSION

COMPREHENSION PROCESSES
Remember, Understand

WRITING TRAITS
Organization—Topic Sentence, Supporting Details
Conventions—Complete Sentence, Capital, Period
Presentation

Identifying—What

Identifying—What

Using Graphic Organizer; Locating Information; Identifying—Supporting Details; Using Vocabulary—energy

Summarizing—Main Idea/Topic
Supporting Details/Facts
Sentence Writing

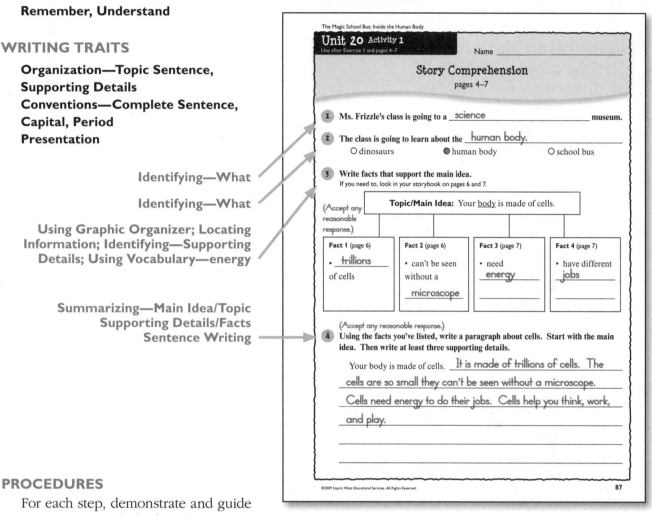

The Magic School Bus: Inside the Human Body

Unit 20 Activity 1
Use after Exercise 1 and pages 4–7

Name _____

Story Comprehension
pages 4–7

1. Ms. Frizzle's class is going to a __science__ museum.

2. The class is going to learn about the __human body.__
   ○ dinosaurs   ● human body   ○ school bus

3. Write facts that support the main idea.
   If you need to, look in your storybook on pages 6 and 7.

   (Accept any reasonable response.)

   Topic/Main Idea: Your <u>body</u> is made of cells.

Fact 1 (page 6)	**Fact 2** (page 6)	**Fact 3** (page 7)	**Fact 4** (page 7)
• __trillions__ of cells	• can't be seen without a __microscope__	• need __energy__	• have different __jobs__

   (Accept any reasonable response.)

4. Using the facts you've listed, write a paragraph about cells. Start with the main idea. Then write at least three supporting details.

   Your body is made of cells. __It is made of trillions of cells. The cells are so small they can't be seen without a microscope. Cells need energy to do their jobs. Cells help you think, work, and play.__

©2009 Sopris West Educational Services. All Rights Reserved.   87

PROCEDURES
For each step, demonstrate and guide practice, as needed. Then have students complete the page independently.

1. **Sentence Completion—Basic Instructions** (Item 1)
   Have students fill in the blank with the correct answer.

2. **Selection Response—Basic Instructions** (Item 2)
   Have students fill in the bubble and blank with the answer.

3. **Main Idea/Supporting Details: Hierarchy Chart—Basic Instructions** (Item 3)
   • Have students read the topic/main idea.
   • Have students complete the facts about cells.

4. **Fact Summary: Paragraph Writing—Specific Instructions** (Item 4)
   Have students write a fact summary paragraph with the facts from Item 3. Assist, only as needed.

Self-monitoring
Have students check and correct their work.

FACT SHEET

COMPREHENSION PROCESSES
Understand, Apply, Create

WRITING TRAITS
Word Choice
Conventions—Capital, Period
Presentation

PROCEDURES
For each step, demonstrate and guide practice, as needed. Then have students complete the page independently.

1. **Title and Author Completion—Specific Instructions**
   - Have students read the title starter and then complete the title with their own word choice. Brainstorm ideas with your students. Say something like:
   Are you surprised by what cells can do? What's a snazzy word we've learned that means surprising in a good way? (amazing) What are some other snazzy words that describe how amazing cells are? (wonderful, splendid, fascinating) Write one of those words to complete the title.
   - Have students write their own name to identify the author.

2. **Illustrating—Specific Instructions**
   Have students look at the illustration of lung cells. Then have students draw muscle and brain cells. Remind students to look in their storybooks to see what muscle and brain cells look like.

3. **Sentence Completion—Specific Instructions**
   Have students select a type of cell and complete the caption at the bottom of the large box.

4. **Illustrating—Specific Instructions**
   Have students visualize and illustrate the caption.

Self-monitoring
Have students check and correct their work.

Generating Ideas—Title

Identifying—Author

Viewing, Locating Information Illustrating

Visualizing Illustrating

Explaining—Fact

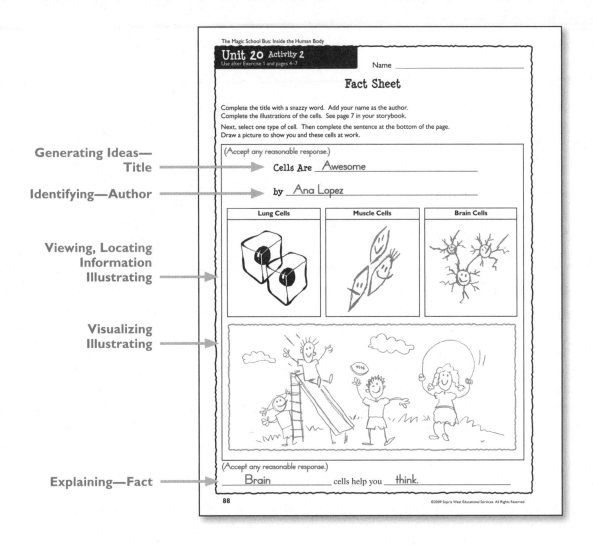

The Magic School Bus: Inside the Human Body

Unit 20 Activity 2
Use after Exercise 1 and pages 4–7

Name _____

Fact Sheet

Complete the title with a snazzy word. Add your name as the author.
Complete the illustrations of the cells. See page 7 in your storybook.

Next, select one type of cell. Then complete the sentence at the bottom of the page.
Draw a picture to show you and these cells at work.

(Accept any reasonable response.)

Cells Are Awesome _____

by Ana Lopez _____

Lung Cells	Muscle Cells	Brain Cells

(Accept any reasonable response.)

_____ Brain _____ cells help you __ think. __

88

❶ SOUND REVIEW

Use selected Sound Cards from Units 1–19.

❷ SOUND PRACTICE

- For each task, have students spell and say the focus sound in the gray bar.
  For Rhyming Words and Bossy <u>E</u>, read the header.
- Next, have students read each underlined sound, the word, then the column.
- Repeat with each column, building accuracy first, then fluency.

❸ ACCURACY AND FLUENCY BUILDING

C1. Multisyllabic Words

- For the list of words divided by syllables, have students read
  each syllable, then the whole word. Use the word in a sentence,
  as appropriate.
- For the list of whole words, build accuracy, then fluency.

esophagus	When you swallow food, it goes down the . . . *esophagus.*
intestine	Food is digested in the . . . *intestine.*
products	Cheese, yogurt, and ice cream are milk . . . *products.*
processor	Dad chops onions in our food . . . *processor.*
ignition	To start a car, you put a key in the . . . *ignition.*
molecules	The smallest parts that make up something are called . . . *molecules.*
Dorothy	Jaqueline's best friend is a girl named . . . *Dorothy.*

D1. Tricky Words

- For each Tricky Word, have students use the sounds and word parts they know to
  silently sound out the word. Use the word in a sentence to help with pronunciation.
- If the word is unfamiliar, tell students the word.

poultry
Look at the first word. The word is *poultry*. Say the word. (poultry)
Birds that are raised for their eggs or meat are . . . *poultry.*
Read the word three times. (poultry, poultry, poultry)

tongue	There are taste buds on our . . . *tongue.*
juices	Orange and apple are two kinds of . . . *juices.*
educational	The book about animals was very . . . *educational.*
research	Some scientists do a lot of . . . *research.*

- Have students go back and read the whole words in the column.

❹ RELATED WORDS

Tell students the words are related to "digest." Have them read the words. Use the words in
sentences, as needed.

❺ MORPHOGRAPHS AND AFFIXES

- Have students read the underlined part, then the whole word.
- Repeat practice with whole words, mixing group and individual turns.
  Build accuracy, then fluency.
- Use the words in sentences, as needed.

> **ACCURACY
> AND FLUENCY
> BUILDING**
> **(Reminder)**
>
> For each task, have
> students say any
> underlined part, then read
> the word.
>
> Set a pace. Then have
> students read the whole
> words in each task and
> column.
>
> Provide repeated practice,
> building accuracy first,
> then fluency.

6 GENERALIZATION: READING NEW WORDS IN PARAGRAPHS

- Have students read the paragraph silently, then out loud. Tell students to use the sounds and word parts they know to read any difficult words.
- Repeat practice, as needed.

The Magic School Bus: Inside the Human Body

Unit 20 Exercise 2
Use before pages 8–13

1. SOUND REVIEW Use selected Sound Cards from Units 1–19.

2. SOUND PRACTICE In each column, have students spell and say the sound, next say any underlined sound and the word, then read the column.

ow as in snow	ou	ur	Rhyming Words	Bossy E
sh<u>ow</u>s	m<u>ou</u>th	ch<u>ur</u>ning	honey	t<u>u</u>be
fl<u>ow</u>s	s<u>ou</u>nd	yog<u>ur</u>t	monkey	n<u>i</u>ce
swall<u>ow</u>	s<u>ou</u>r	t<u>ur</u>ning	key	tr<u>a</u>de

3. ACCURACY/FLUENCY BUILDING For each column, have students say any underlined part, then read each word. Next, have them read the column.

A1 Mixed Practice	B1 Word Endings	C1 Multisyllabic Words		D1 Tricky Words
buds	<u>broken</u>	e•soph•a•gus	esophagus	poultry
slight	gases	in•tes•tine	intestine	tongue
grain	<u>divided</u>	prod•ucts	products	juices
ick	<u>strangest</u>	pro•ces•sor	processor	educational
cells	<u>detecting</u>	ig•ni•tion	ignition	research
<u>Phil</u>		mol•e•cules	molecules	
	gurgle	Dor•o•thy	Dorothy	
	gurgling			

4. RELATED WORDS Have students read the words.

digests	digested	digestive	digestion

5. MORPHOGRAPHS AND AFFIXES Have students read the underlined part, then the word.

Ⓐ	ac<u>tion</u>s	atten<u>tion</u>	be<u>hind</u>	e<u>x</u>actly
Ⓑ	terrif<u>ic</u>	bottom<u>less</u>	thick<u>ness</u>	horr<u>ible</u>

6. GENERALIZATION Have students read the paragraph silently, then out loud. (New words: Wanda, daydream, Cheesie-Weesies, cereal, pasta)

As usual, Wanda was very hungry after soccer practice. Her stomach was growling. She began to daydream about yummy foods. "What can I eat?" she thought. "Cheesie-Weesies? No, something healthy. Cereal and milk? That would be okay. Hmmm, pasta and vegetables? Yes, that would be great."

BUILDING MASTERY WITH JAZZY PRACTICE (Reminder)

For variety, practice underlined sounds in a jazzy rhythm. Say something like:

Listen to me read Column A1 in a rhythm. I'm going to quickly say each underlined sound two times and then read the word.

/ŭ/, /ŭ/, buds;
/ī/, /ī/, slight;
/ā/, /ā/, grain.

Your turn. Start at the top of Column A1 and keep going.
(/ŭ/, /ŭ/, buds;
/ī/, /ī/, slight;
/ā/, /ā/, grain.)

GENTLE CORRECTIONS (Reminder)

If you hear an error, write the word on the board.

Have all students identify the difficult sound and then blend the word.

Periodically, repeat practice of the difficult word.

67

COMPREHENSION PROCESSES

Understand, Apply

PROCEDURES

1. Introducing Vocabulary

★ **daydream** ★ **liquid** ★ **break down** ★ **upset**

- For each vocabulary word, have students read the word by parts, then read the whole word.
- Read the student-friendly explanations to students as they follow with their fingers. Then have students use the vocabulary word by following the gray text.
- Review and discuss the illustrations.
  Note: Student vocabulary pages for this unit are found in the students' *Exercise Book 3*.

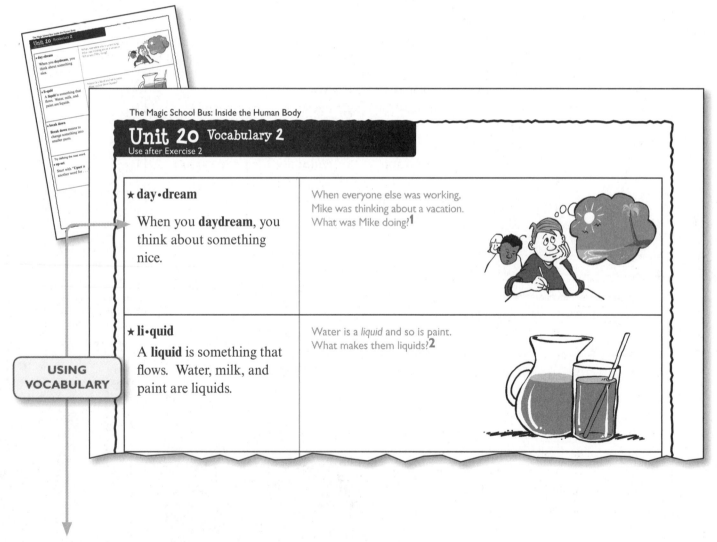

USING VOCABULARY

The Magic School Bus: Inside the Human Body

Unit 20 Vocabulary 2
Use after Exercise 2

★ **day·dream**

When you **daydream**, you think about something nice.

When everyone else was working, Mike was thinking about a vacation. What was Mike doing?[1]

★ **li·quid**

A **liquid** is something that flows. Water, milk, and paint are liquids.

Water is a *liquid* and so is paint. What makes them liquids?[2]

---

❶ **Apply:** Using Vocabulary—daydream (Mike was daydreaming.)

❷ **Understand:** Defining and Using Vocabulary—liquid (Water and paint both flow, so they are liquids.)

★ = New in this unit

2. Now You Try It!

- Have students read the last word by parts and then read the whole word.
- Have students explain or define the word in their own words, then use the word in a sentence.

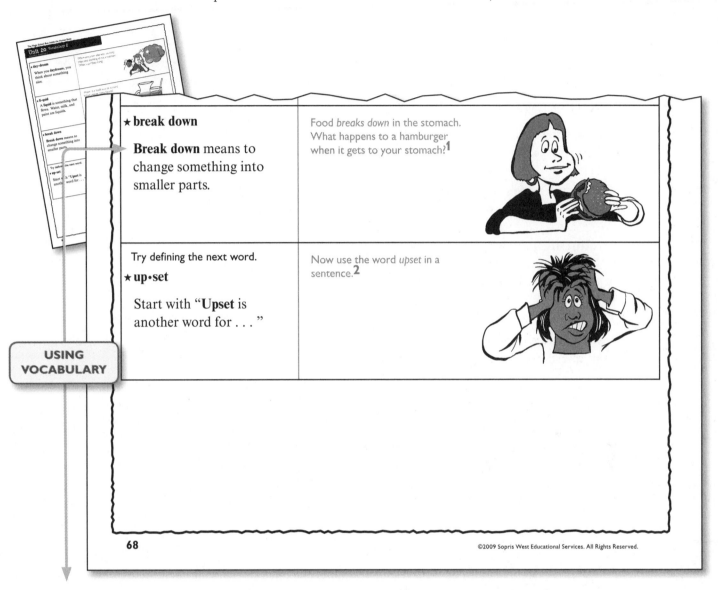

USING VOCABULARY

★ **break down**

Break down means to change something into smaller parts.

Food *breaks down* in the stomach. What happens to a hamburger when it gets to your stomach?[1]

Try defining the next word.

★ **up•set**

Start with "**Upset** is another word for . . ."

Now use the word *upset* in a sentence.[2]

68

©2009 Sopris West Educational Services. All Rights Reserved.

1 Apply: Using Vocabulary—break down (The hamburger changes into smaller parts. The hamburger breaks down in the stomach.)

2 Understand: Defining and/or Using Vocabulary—upset, distressed (Upset is another word for distressed. I got upset when I couldn't find my homework.)

STORY READING INSTRUCTIONS

Students read pages 8–11 with the teacher and pages 12 and 13 on their own.

COMPREHENSION PROCESSES

Remember, Understand, Apply

PROCEDURES

1. Reviewing pages 4–7

Summarizing; Identifying—What, Where

Turn to page 4. Review how the story started.

Pages four to seven introduced us to the story.

What is Ms. Frizzle's class going to study? (They will study the human body.)

Where are they going to go? (They are going to the science museum.)

2. Introducing pages 8–13

Say something like:

I like reading the fact sheets that Ms. Frizzle's kids are writing.

They are smart like you! Let's see what Arnold wrote.

3. First Reading

- Ask questions and discuss the story as indicated by the blue text in this guide.
- Mix group and individual turns, independent of your voice.
  Have students work toward a group accuracy goal of 0–6 errors.
  Quietly keep track of errors made by all students in the group.
- After reading the story, practice any difficult words.
  Reread the story if students have not reached the accuracy goal.

After Reading Page 8: Your Mouth Has Thousands of Taste Buds!

❶ **Remember:** Identifying—Facts
What did Arnold find out about taste buds?
(There are thousands of taste buds on your tongue. Different parts of the tongue taste different things.)

After Reading Page 8

❷ **Remember:** Identifying—Event
What was the class doing on this page?
(They were on their field trip. They stopped at a park for lunch.)

❸ **Apply:** Inferring, Explaining; **Understand:** Using Vocabulary—trade
Why does Arnold say he'll trade his "terrific fish sticks for that horrible peanut butter and banana sandwich"?
(He wants someone to think the fish sticks are tasty, so they'll trade him lunches.)

After Reading Page 9

1 **Understand:** Explaining—Facts; Defining and/or Using Vocabulary—digest, energy
What does your body do with food?
(It digests it.)
That means that food is broken down into smaller parts so it can be used to make energy. What does the body do when it digests food?
(Your body breaks it down to make energy.)

2 **Remember:** Identifying—Facts; Using Vocabulary—energy
Read Carmen's report again. What did you learn?
(You need to eat healthy food to have energy and grow. You need to eat a lot of bread, cereal, pasta, veggies, and fruits. You also need milk, meat, poultry, eggs, fish, and fats.)

"Hurry up, Arnold!" called Ms. Frizzle. She reached for the ignition key, but instead she pushed a strange little button nearby.

At once, we started shrinking and spinning through the air.

From inside, we couldn't see what was happening. All we knew was that we landed suddenly...

and then we were going down a dark tunnel.
We had no idea where we were.
But, as usual, Ms. Frizzle knew.
She said we were inside a human body,
going down the esophagus—
the tube that leads from the mouth
to the stomach.
Most of us were too upset
about leaving Arnold behind
to pay much attention.

WHERE'S ARNOLD?

HE GOT LEFT!

THAT'S WHAT HAPPENS WHEN YOU EAT JUNK FOOD!

I THOUGHT WE WERE GOING TO THE MUSEUM.

THERE'S BEEN A SLIGHT CHANGE OF PLANS... WE'RE BEING DIGESTED INSTEAD.

FOOD GOES TO YOUR STOMACH THROUGH THE ESOPHAGUS
by Wanda
The food does not just fall down. It is pushed along by muscle actions the way toothpaste is squeezed out of a tube. That's why you can swallow even when you are upside down.

MUSCLES SQUEEZE TO PUSH FOOD TO YOUR STOMACH

11

STORY READING INSTRUCTIONS

Students read pages 12 and 13 without the teacher, independently or with partners.

COMPREHENSION PROCESSES

Remember, Understand, Apply

PROCEDURES

1. Getting Ready

Have students turn to page 12.

2. Setting a Purpose

Inferring; Explaining; Identifying—Where; Using Vocabulary—absurd; Explaining—Facts

Before students begin reading, say something like:

As you read the next pages, try to answer these questions:

• At the end of the section, why did the bird call Arnold a "poor kid"?
• Where did the magic school bus take the kids?
• What is absurd about this story?
• What facts did you learn about swallowing?

3. Reading on Your Own: Partner or Whisper Reading

• Have students take turns reading every other page with a partner or have students whisper read pages 12 and 13 on their own.
• Continue having students track each word with their fingers.

4. Comprehension and Skill Work

Tell students that they will do Comprehension and Skill Activity 3 and work on The Human Body Cover and Entry 1 after they read on their own. Guide practice, as needed. For teacher directions, see pages 40 and 41.

5. Homework 2: New Passage

STORY COMPREHENSION

MAZE READING

COMPREHENSION PROCESSES

Understand, Apply

WRITING TRAITS

Period

Identifying—Who

Locating Information; Viewing
Explaining—Events; Inferring

Inferring

Comprehension Monitoring, Test Taking

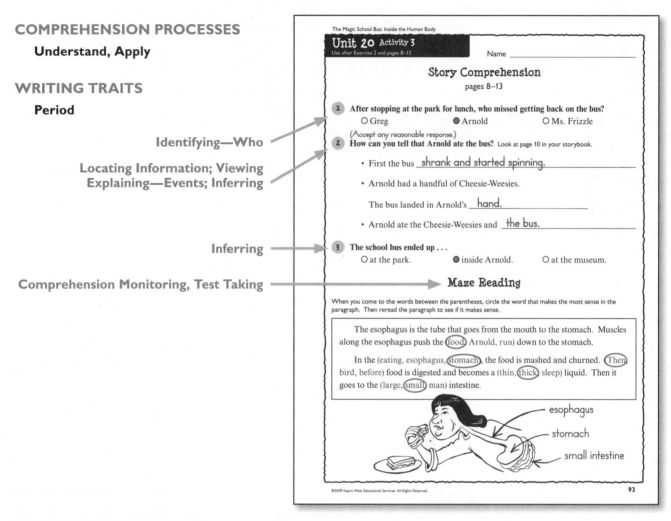

The Magic School Bus: Inside the Human Body

Unit 20 Activity 3
Use after Exercise 2 and pages 8–13

Name _____

Story Comprehension
pages 8–13

1. After stopping at the park for lunch, who missed getting back on the bus?
   ○ Greg   ● Arnold   ○ Ms. Frizzle
   (Accept any reasonable response.)

2. How can you tell that Arnold ate the bus? Look at page 10 in your storybook.
   • First the bus __shrank and started spinning.__
   • Arnold had a handful of Cheesie-Weesies.
     The bus landed in Arnold's __hand.__
   • Arnold ate the Cheesie-Weesies and __the bus.__

3. The school bus ended up . . .
   ○ at the park.   ● inside Arnold.   ○ at the museum.

Maze Reading

When you come to the words between the parentheses, circle the word that makes the most sense in the paragraph. Then reread the paragraph to see if it makes sense.

The esophagus is the tube that goes from the mouth to the stomach. Muscles along the esophagus push the (food, Arnold, run) down to the stomach.

In the (eating, esophagus, stomach), the food is mashed and churned. (Then, bird, before) food is digested and becomes a (thin, thick, sleep) liquid. Then it goes to the (large, small, man) intestine.

— esophagus
— stomach
— small intestine

93

PROCEDURES

For each step, demonstrate and guide practice, as needed. Then have students complete the page independently.

Story Comprehension

1. **Selection Response—Basic Instructions** (Items 1, 3)
   Have students read the question or sentence starter, then fill in the bubble or blank with the answer.

2. **Sentence Completion—Basic Instructions** (Item 2)
   Have students read the sentence starters, then fill in the blanks. Remind them to put a period at the end of a sentence.

Maze Reading—Basic Instructions

Have students read the paragraphs and select the word in the parentheses that best completes each sentence.

Self-monitoring

Have students check and correct their work.

COVER AND ENTRY 1

COMPREHENSION PROCESSES
Understand

WRITING TRAITS
Conventions—Complete Sentence, Capital, Period

Illustrating; Using Graphic Organizer; Viewing; Explaining—Fact; Sentence Writing

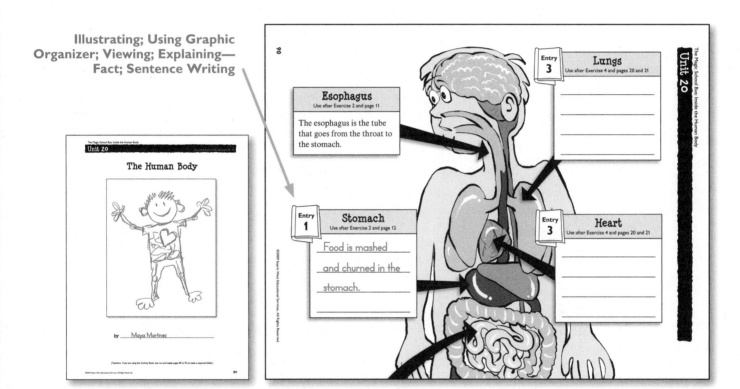

PROCEDURES
Have students complete the page independently. Guide practice, only as needed.

1. Preparation
After pages 89–82 have been removed from *Activity Book 3*, have students write their names on the cover.

2. Cover: Illustrating
Have students design their own cover.

3. Human Body: Diagram, Caption Writing—Specific Instructions
- Have students look at the diagram of the human body.
- Have students read the caption for "esophagus."
- Have students write a short caption about the stomach. Remind students that they can look at storybook page 12 for information about the stomach.
- Remind them to use a complete sentence, capitals, and a period.

> **SPECIAL NOTE**
>
> Across the unit, your students will complete a human body diagram. For ease of use, pull pages 89–92 from *Activity Book 3*. Tape the pages down the center to create a folder.

① SOUND REVIEW

Have students read the sounds and key word phrases. Work for accuracy, then fluency.

② ACCURACY AND FLUENCY BUILDING

C1. Multisyllabic Words

- For the list of words divided by syllables, have students read each syllable, then the whole word. Use the word in a sentence, as appropriate.
- For the list of whole words, build accuracy, then fluency.

pipelines	People heat their homes with gas that travels through . . . *pipelines.*
delivery	Trucks that deliver goods are called . . . *delivery . . .* trucks.
plasma	A yellowish liquid that is part of blood is . . . *plasma.*
platelets	Another part of blood is . . . *platelets.*
intestines	People have small and large . . . *intestines.*
controlled	The bus driver opened the door with the handle that . . . *controlled . . .* it.
oxygen	Part of what makes up the air we breathe is . . . *oxygen.*

D1. Tricky Words

- For each Tricky Word, have students use the sounds and word parts they know to silently sound out the word. Use the word in a sentence to help with pronunciation.

soldiers	The men and women who protect us from our enemies are called . . . *soldiers.*
blood	Dad likes to help the hospital by donating . . . *blood.*
bloodstream	Oxygen is carried throughout the body by the . . . *bloodstream.*
stomach	Food is churned and mashed in your . . . *stomach.*

- Have students go back and read the whole words in the column.

③ WORDS IN CONTEXT

For each word, have students use the sounds and word parts they know to silently sound out the word. Then have students read the sentence. Assist, as needed.

④ MORPHOGRAPHS AND AFFIXES

- Have students read the underlined part, then the word.
- Repeat practice with whole words, mixing group and individual turns. Build accuracy, then fluency.

⑤ GENERALIZATION: READING NEW WORDS IN PARAGRAPHS

- Have students read the paragraph silently, then out loud. Tell students to use the sounds and word parts they know to read any difficult words.
- Repeat practice, as needed.

> **ACCURACY AND FLUENCY BUILDING (Reminder)**
>
> For each task, have students say any underlined part, then read the word.
>
> Set a pace. Then have students read the whole words in each task and column.
>
> Provide repeated practice, building accuracy first, then fluency.

The Magic School Bus: Inside the Human Body

Unit 20 Exercise 3
Use before pages 14–19

1. SOUND REVIEW Have students review sounds for accuracy, then for fluency.

Ⓐ	o as in open	ow as in snow	igh as in flight	i as in silent	or as in horn
Ⓑ	ph	ge	kn	ue	ci

2. ACCURACY/FLUENCY BUILDING For each column, have students say any underlined part, then read each word. Next, have them read the column.

A1 Mixed Practice	B1 Word Endings	C1 Multisyllabic Words		D1 Tricky Words
c<u>o</u>iled	<u>germs</u>	pipe·lines	pipelines	soldiers
Molly	<u>saucers</u>	de·liv·er·y	delivery	blood
gl<u>i</u>mpse		plas·ma	plasma	bloodstream
holl<u>ow</u>	chase	plate·lets	platelets	stomach
<u>a</u>dult	chasing	in·tes·tines	intestines	
	enemy	con·trolled	controlled	
	enemies	ox·y·gen	oxygen	

3. WORDS IN CONTEXT Have students use the sounds and word parts they know to figure out each word. Then have them read each sentence.

Ⓐ	vil·li	<u>Villi</u> are small finger-like things on the walls of intestines.
Ⓑ	ves·sel	A blood <u>vessel</u> is a tube in your body that carries blood.
Ⓒ	me·ter	A <u>meter</u> is a measurement that is equal to about three feet.
Ⓓ	flu·id	Water and juice are each a <u>fluid</u>. Fluids are like liquids.

4. MORPHOGRAPHS AND AFFIXES Have students read the underlined part, then the word.

<u>de</u>stroying	<u>dis</u>gusting	<u>ex</u>plained	pan<u>ic</u>	stretch<u>able</u>

5. GENERALIZATION Have students read the paragraph silently, then out loud. (New words: Shirley, disease)

   This plant does not look healthy. Its leaves are yellowish instead of green. My friend Shirley says it might have a disease. I will try my best to make it healthy again.

69

APPROPRIATE CORRECTIONS
(Reminder)

Write any difficult words on a board or clipboard.

Single-Syllable Pattern Words

Have students identify the difficult sound, then sound out and say the word.

Multisyllabic Words

Draw loops under each word part and then guide practice with your hand.

Tricky Words

Have students sound out or read the word by parts, then say the word. Next have students say, spell, and say the word.

After gently correcting a word with the group, go on to other tasks or words. Return to the difficult word at least three times.

COMPREHENSION PROCESSES

Understand, Apply

PROCEDURES

1. **Introducing Vocabulary**

⭐waste ⭐fluid ⭐oxygen ⭐swept out ⭐glimpse, panic ⭐esophagus

- For each vocabulary word, have students read the word by parts, then read the whole word.
- Read the student-friendly explanations to students as they follow with their fingers. Then have students use the vocabulary word by following the gray text.
- Review and discuss the illustrations.
  Note: Student vocabulary pages for this unit are found in the students' *Exercise Book 3*.

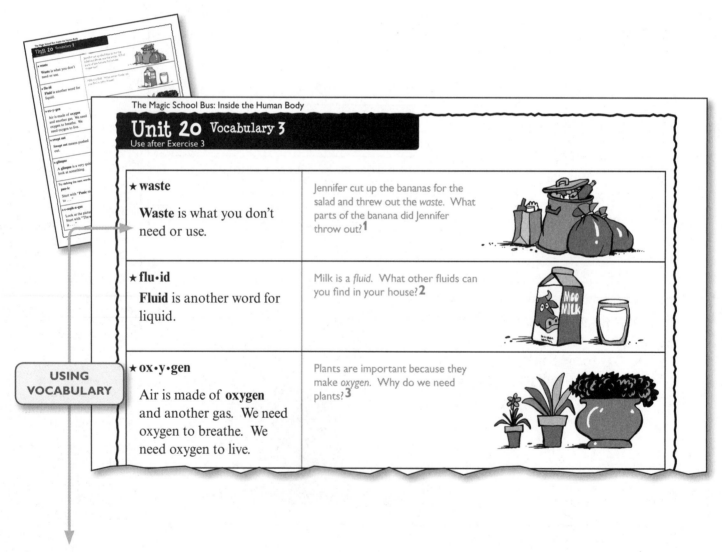

USING
VOCABULARY

The Magic School Bus: Inside the Human Body

Unit 20 Vocabulary 3
Use after Exercise 3

★ **waste** **Waste** is what you don't need or use.	Jennifer cut up the bananas for the salad and threw out the *waste*. What parts of the banana did Jennifer throw out?**1**
★ **flu·id** **Fluid** is another word for liquid.	Milk is a *fluid*. What other fluids can you find in your house?**2**
★ **ox·y·gen** Air is made of **oxygen** and another gas. We need oxygen to breathe. We need oxygen to live.	Plants are important because they make *oxygen*. Why do we need plants?**3**

❶ **Understand:** Using Vocabulary—waste (She threw out the banana peels. She threw out the waste.)
❷ **Apply:** Using Vocabulary—fluid (Juice, soda, and laundry soap are fluids in my house.)
❸ **Apply:** Using Vocabulary—oxygen (We need plants because they make oxygen.)

⭐ = New in this unit

2. Now You Try It!
- Have students read the last two words by parts and then read the whole word.
- Have students explain or define the words in their own words, then use the words in a sentence.

USING
VOCABULARY

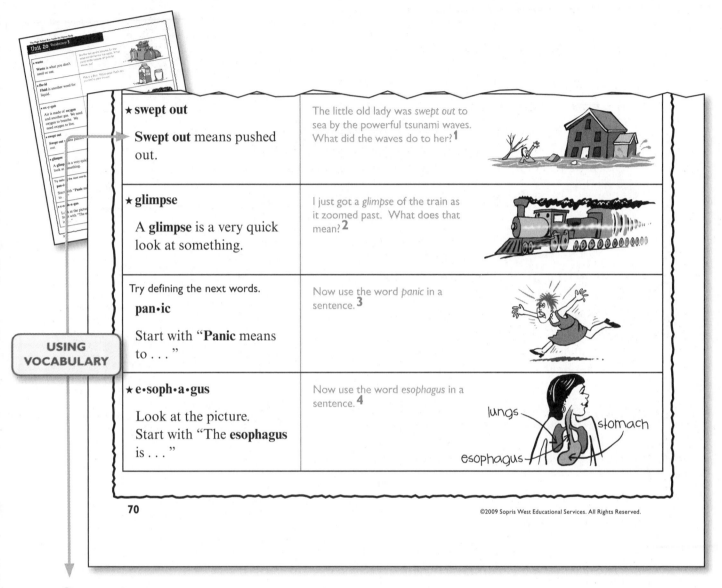

★ **swept out** **Swept out** means pushed out.	The little old lady was *swept out* to sea by the powerful tsunami waves. What did the waves do to her?[1]
★ **glimpse** A **glimpse** is a very quick look at something.	I just got a *glimpse* of the train as it zoomed past. What does that mean?[2]
Try defining the next words. **pan·ic** Start with "**Panic** means to . . ."	Now use the word *panic* in a sentence.[3]
★ **e·soph·a·gus** Look at the picture. Start with "The **esophagus** is . . ."	Now use the word *esophagus* in a sentence.[4]

70

❶ **Apply:** Using Vocabulary—swept out (The waves pushed the little old lady out to sea.)

❷ **Understand:** Defining and Using Vocabulary—glimpse (It means you got a very quick look at the train.)

❸ **Understand:** Defining and Using Vocabulary—panic, frantic (Panic means to suddenly feel frightened. I panic sometimes when I can't find my cat. When someone panics, he or she is frantic.)

❹ **Understand:** Defining and Using Vocabulary—esophagus (The esophagus is the tube that goes from your mouth to your stomach. A piece of apple got stuck in my esophagus.)

STORY READING INSTRUCTIONS

Students read pages 14–17 with the teacher and pages 18 and 19 on their own.

COMPREHENSION PROCESSES

Remember, Understand, Apply

PROCEDURES

1. **Reviewing pages 12 and 13**

   Summarizing; Identifying—Where; Using Vocabulary—absurd, esophagus, liquid, break down; Locating Information; Explaining—Facts

   Quickly review the questions from the previous Setting a Purpose. Say something like:

   Yesterday, you read pages 12 and 13 on your own. Let's see what you found out. At the end of this section, why did the bird call Arnold a "poor kid"?
   (Arnold was sick to his stomach. He had a school bus inside him . . .)
   Where did the magic school bus take the kids?
   (It went down Arnold's esophagus into his stomach and his small intestines.)
   What is absurd about this story?
   (A school bus could never shrink like that and go inside a body. You couldn't really take a trip through the human body.)
   Those things would be fun, but crazy . . . They couldn't really happen.
   They are definitely absurd.
   What facts did you learn about swallowing?
   Let's look through your book. It will help you remember what you learned.
   (Food goes down a tube called the esophagus. Muscles push food into your stomach. The stomach mashes and churns the food into a liquid. Then it moves into your small intestine where it breaks down . . .)

   > **CORRECTING DECODING ERRORS**
   >
   > During story reading, gently correct any error, then have students reread the sentence.

2. **Introducing pages 14–17**

   Viewing, Predicting

   Look at the picture on page 14. Where do you think the bus is going next?

3. **First Reading**
   - Ask questions and discuss the story as indicated by the blue text in this guide.
   - Mix group and individual turns, independent of your voice.
     Have students work toward a group accuracy goal of 0–6 errors.
     Quietly keep track of errors made by all students in the group.
   - After reading the story, practice any difficult words.
     Reread the story if students have not reached the accuracy goal.

4. **Second Reading, Short Passage Practice: Developing Prosody**
   - Demonstrate expressive, fluent reading of the first two paragraphs.
   - Guide practice with your voice.
   - Provide individual turns while others track with their fingers and whisper read.
   - Repeat with one paragraph at a time.

After Reading Page 14: Why Are the Intestines Coiled Up?

❶ Understand: Explaining—Fact
Why are the intestines coiled up?
(They are about 25 feet long. They have to be coiled to fit inside our body. If they were stretched out, we would have to be 25 feet tall.)

After Reading Page 14

❷ Understand: Explaining; Using Vocabulary—absurd
Is there anything absurd happening in this part of the story?
(Yes, the bus is getting even smaller and driving into a blood vessel.)

❸ Apply: Predicting
Ms. Frizzle said, "Once the food is in the blood, it can travel all over the body." Where do you think the kids will go next?
(I think they will travel all over the body.)

**COMPREHENSION BUILDING
(Reminder)**

Encourage students to answer questions with complete sentences. If students have difficulty comprehending, think aloud with them or reread the portion of the story that answers the question. Then repeat the question.

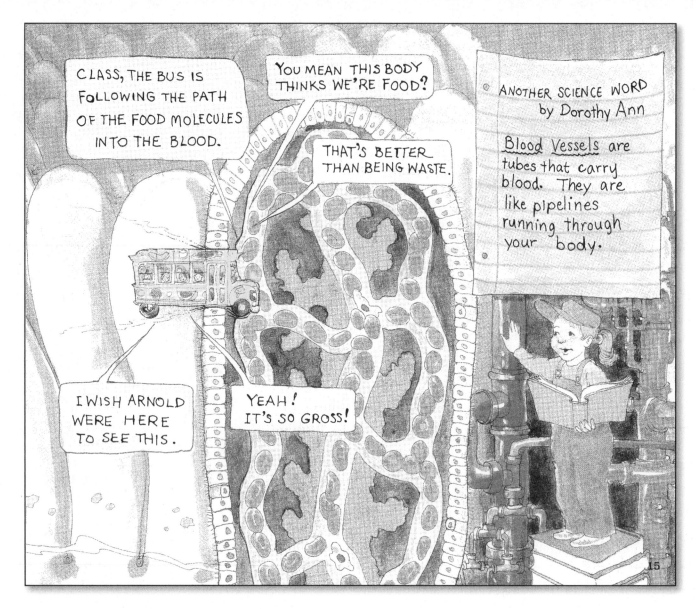

After Reading Page 15

❶ **Apply:** Inferring, Explaining
Where is the bus going?
(The bus is going into the blood vessels.)

❷ **Understand:** Explaining—Fact
What are blood vessels?
(Blood vessels are tubes that carry blood.)

❸ **Apply:** Inferring; Explaining
Do you think the kids are having fun?
(Most of them probably are. It's an exciting experience that no one else has ever had . . .)

After Reading Page 16: What Is Blood Made of?

❶ Understand: Explaining—Fact
Name three things that blood is made of.
(Blood is made of plasma, cells, and platelets.)

After Reading Page 16

❷ Remember: Identifying—What
What are the red saucer-like things?
(They are red blood cells.)

❸ Understand: Explaining—Fact
What do the red blood cells do?
(They carry oxygen to other parts of the body.)

After Reading Page 17

❶ Understand: Explaining; **Apply:** Inferring; Using Vocabulary—destroy
Why are white blood cells important?
(They destroy germs that make you get diseases. They keep you from getting sick.)

❷ Understand: Explaining—Fact
Why are platelets important?
(They help you stop bleeding.)

❸ Apply: Inferring
What do you think would happen if you didn't have enough platelets?
(If you cut yourself, it would be hard to stop the bleeding.)

STORY READING INSTRUCTIONS

Students read pages 18 and 19 without the teacher, independently or with partners.

COMPREHENSION PROCESSES

Remember, Understand

PROCEDURES

1. **Getting Ready**

   Have students turn to page 18.

2. **Setting a Purpose**

   Explaining; Identifying—What; Using Vocabulary—panic

   Before students begin reading, say something like:

   On your own, read to find out the answers to these questions:

   • Why was the white blood cell chasing the bus?
   • What did the kids hitch a ride on?
   • Why did Arnold begin to panic?

3. **Reading on Your Own: Partner or Whisper Reading**

   • Have students take turns reading every other page with a partner or have students whisper read pages 18 and 19 on their own.
   • Continue having students track each word with their fingers.

4. **Comprehension and Skill Work**

   Tell students that they will do Comprehension and Skill Activity 4 and work on The Human Body Entry 2 after they read on their own. Guide practice, as needed. For teacher directions, see pages 54 and 55.

5. **Homework 3: New Passage**

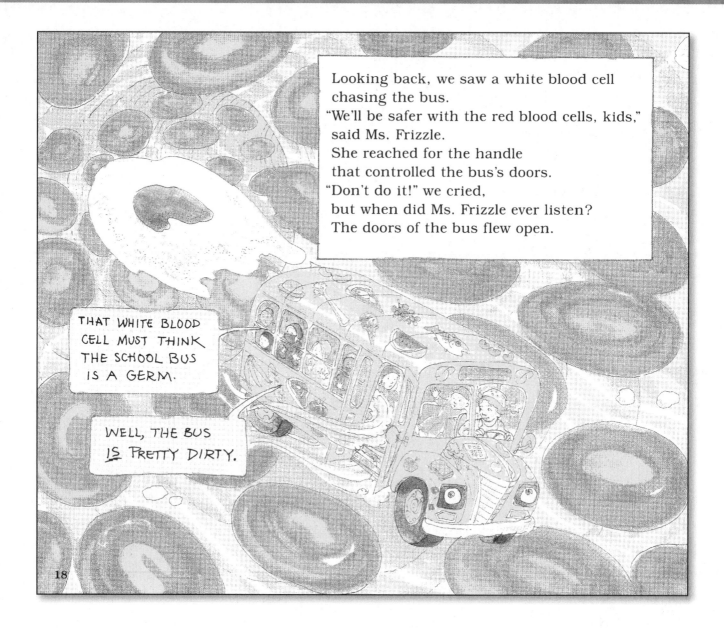

STORY COMPREHENSION

COMPREHENSION PROCESSES
Remember, Understand

WRITING TRAITS
Period

Using Graphic Organizer; Sequencing

Using Graphic Organizer; Locating Information; Identifying—What Using Vocabulary—esophagus

Defining, Sentence Completion

Summarizing—Supporting Details/ Facts; Making Lists, Locating Information

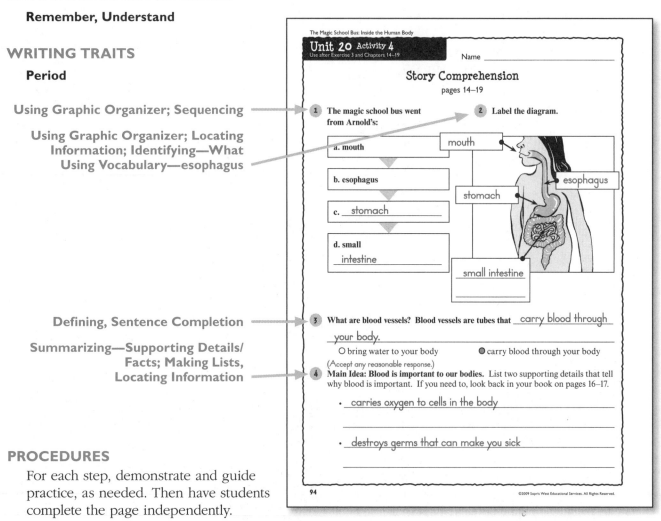

The Magic School Bus: Inside the Human Body

Unit 20 Activity 4
Use after Exercise 3 and Chapters 14–19

Name _____

Story Comprehension
pages 14–19

1. The magic school bus went from Arnold's:

a. mouth

b. esophagus

c. __stomach__

d. small __intestine__

2. Label the diagram.

mouth

esophagus

stomach

small intestine

3. What are blood vessels? Blood vessels are tubes that __carry blood through__ __your body.__
   ○ bring water to your body   ● carry blood through your body
   (Accept any reasonable response.)

4. **Main Idea: Blood is important to our bodies.** List two supporting details that tell why blood is important. If you need to, look back in your book on pages 16–17.
   • __carries oxygen to cells in the body__

   • __destroys germs that can make you sick__

94   ©2009 Sopris West Educational Services. All Rights Reserved.

PROCEDURES
For each step, demonstrate and guide practice, as needed. Then have students complete the page independently.

1. **Sequence of Events Chart—Specific Instructions** (Item 1)
   Have students sequence where the school bus traveled by filling in the blanks with the correct body parts.

2. **Diagram: Labeling—Specific Instructions** (Item 2)
   Have students label the diagram with the correct body parts. Remind students that they can look in their storybooks or at the sequencing chart in Item 1 for the answers.

3. **Selection Response—Basic Instructions** (Item 3)
   Have students read the question and sentence starter, then fill in the bubble and blank to complete the sentence.

4. **Main Idea/Supporting Details—Specific Instructions** (Item 4)
   Have students list two facts that tell why blood is important. Have students look back in their storybooks on pages 16 and 17.

Self-monitoring
Have students check and correct their work.

ENTRY 2

COMPREHENSION PROCESSES

Understand, Apply

WRITING TRAITS

Conventions—Complete Sentence, Capital, Period

Using Graphic Organizer
Viewing; Explaining—Facts
Sentence Writing

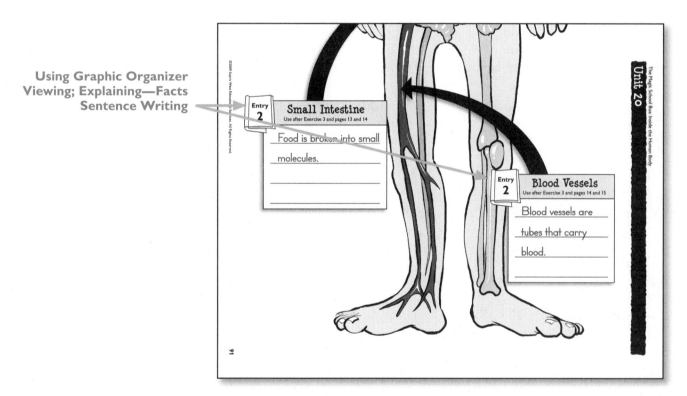

PROCEDURES

Have students complete the page independently. Guide practice, only as needed.

Human Body: Diagram, Caption Writing—Specific Instructions
- Have students look at the diagram of the human body.
- Have students write a short caption about the small intestine. Remind students that they can look at storybook pages 13 and 14 for information on the small intestine.
- Have students write a short caption about blood vessels. Remind students that they can look at storybook pages 14 and 15 for information about blood vessels.
- Remind students to use a complete sentence, capitals, and a period.

❶ SOUND REVIEW

Use selected Sound Cards from Units 1–19.

❷ ACCURACY AND FLUENCY BUILDING

- For each task, have students say any underlined part, then read the word.
- Set a pace. Then have students read the whole words in each task and column.
- Provide repeated practice, building accuracy first, then fluency.

C1. Multisyllabic Words

- For the list of words divided by syllables, have students read each syllable, then the whole word. Use the word in a sentence, as appropriate.
- For the list of whole words, build accuracy, then fluency.

oxygen	Living things need to breathe . . . *oxygen.*
chambers	The heart has four . . . *chambers.*
hollow	The bat hid in the . . . *hollow* . . . of the tree.
carbon dioxide	We breathe in oxygen. We breathe out . . . *carbon dioxide.*

D1. Tricky Words

- For each Tricky Word, have students use the sounds and word parts they know to silently sound out the word. Use the word in a sentence to help with pronunciation.

heart	Exercise helps you have a healthy . . . *heart.*
minute	Sixty seconds equals one . . . *minute.*
hey	When you want someone's attention, you can say . . . *hey.*
school	You get to see all your classmates at . . . *school.*

- Have students go back and read the whole words in the column.

❸ WORD ENDINGS

Have students read the underlined word, then the word with an ending.

❹ RELATED WORDS

Tell students these words have a meaning and spelling related to the word "circles." Use the words in sentences, as needed.

We're going to read words that are related to the word *circles.*

Put your finger on the first word. Read the word. (circles) To go around and around means to circle. The runner circles the track.

Read the next word. (circulate)

To circulate means to move around and around within a place. Help me complete this sentence. The teacher will . . . *circulate* . . . through the classroom to see that we are all working hard.

Read the next word. (circulating) In our bodies right now, blood is . . . *circulating.* Read the last word. (circulation) Exercise helps improve one's . . . *circulation.*

❺ MORPHOGRAPHS AND AFFIXES

- Have students read the underlined part, then the word.
- Repeat practice with whole words, mixing group and individual turns. Build accuracy, then fluency.

⑥ GENERALIZATION: READING NEW WORDS IN PARAGRAPHS

- Have students read the paragraph silently, then out loud. Tell students to use the sounds and word parts they know to read any difficult words.
- Repeat practice, as needed.

The Magic School Bus: Inside the Human Body

Unit 20 Exercise 4
Use before pages 20–23

BUILDING INDEPENDENCE (Reminder)

Some students will try to follow your voice instead of learning to read the sounds and words. Therefore, it is important for you to demonstrate and guide practice only as needed.

Give students many opportunities to respond without your assistance—with groups and individuals. Encourage independence.

1. SOUND REVIEW Use selected Sound Cards from Units 1–19.

2. ACCURACY/FLUENCY BUILDING For each column, have students say any underlined part, then read each word. Next, have them read the column.

A1 Mixed Review	B1 Mixed Practice	C1 Multisyllabic Words		D1 Tricky Words
throw	br<u>ai</u>n	ox•y•gen	oxygen	heart
strict	br<u>ea</u>th	cham•bers	chambers	minute
sac	fr<u>e</u>sh	hol•low	hollow	hey
squeeze	w<u>a</u>ste	car•bon di•ox•ide	carbon dioxide	school

3. WORD ENDINGS Have students read each underlined word, then the word with an ending.

<u>pound</u>ing	<u>flow</u>ed	<u>pump</u>s	<u>lung</u>s

4. RELATED WORDS Have students read the words.

circles	circulate	circulating	circulation

5. MORPHOGRAPHS AND AFFIXES Have students read the underlined part, then the word.

<u>refresh</u>	move<u>ment</u>	un<u>less</u>	round<u>ness</u>

6. GENERALIZATION Have students read the paragraph silently, then out loud. (New words: Florrie, plastic)

Florrie knows that it is important to recycle. She made a sign and put it up on the bulletin board at school. Since Florrie put her sign up, kids at her school have recycled twice as much as before. They remind their parents to recycle too.

HELP THE EARTH!

Recycle your cans and plastic bottles

71

57

COMPREHENSION PROCESSES

Understand, Apply

PROCEDURES

Introducing Vocabulary

⭐**have a heart** ⭐**get rid of** ⭐**circulate** ⭐**circulation** ⭐**unless**

- For each vocabulary word, have students read the word by parts, then read the whole word.
- Read the student-friendly explanations to students as they follow with their fingers. Then have students use the vocabulary word by following the gray text.
- Review and discuss the illustrations.
  Note: Student vocabulary pages for this unit are found in the students' *Exercise Book 3*.

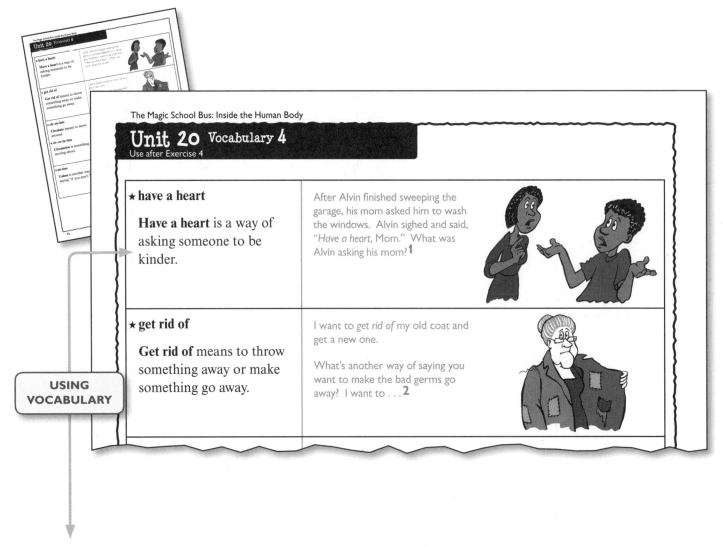

USING VOCABULARY

The Magic School Bus: Inside the Human Body

Unit 20 Vocabulary **4**
Use after Exercise 4

★ **have a heart**

Have a heart is a way of asking someone to be kinder.

After Alvin finished sweeping the garage, his mom asked him to wash the windows. Alvin sighed and said, "*Have a heart*, Mom." What was Alvin asking his mom?**1**

★ **get rid of**

Get rid of means to throw something away or make something go away.

I want to *get rid of* my old coat and get a new one.

What's another way of saying you want to make the bad germs go away? I want to . . .**2**

❶ **Understand:** Defining and Using Idioms and Expressions—have a heart (Alvin was asking his mom to be kinder, to let him rest, to give him a break . . .)

❷ **Apply:** Using Idioms and Expressions—get rid of (get rid of the bad germs)

⭐ = New in this unit

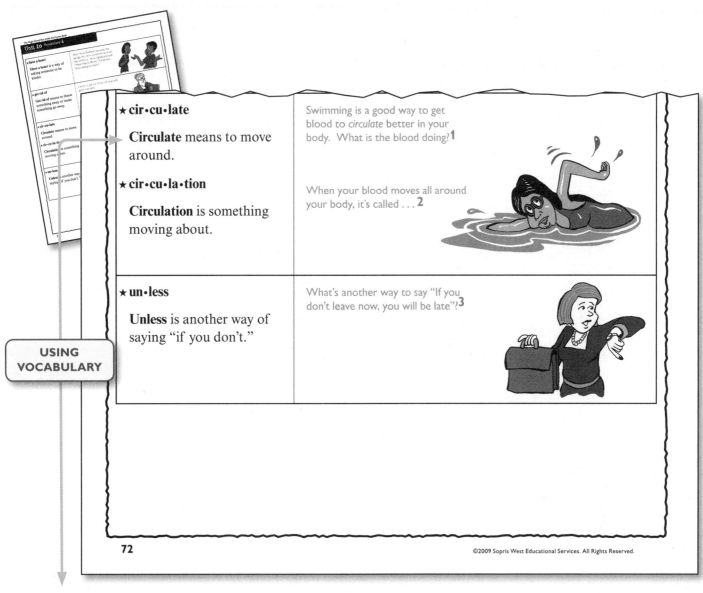

USING
VOCABULARY

★ **cir·cu·late**

Circulate means to move around.

★ **cir·cu·la·tion**

Circulation is something moving about.

Swimming is a good way to get blood to *circulate* better in your body. What is the blood doing?**1**

When your blood moves all around your body, it's called . . . **2**

★ **un·less**

Unless is another way of saying "if you don't."

What's another way to say "If you don't leave now, you will be late"?**3**

72

❶ **Understand:** Defining and Using Vocabulary—circulate (The blood is moving around.)

❷ **Apply:** Using Vocabulary—circulation (circulation)

❸ **Apply:** Using Vocabulary—unless (Unless you leave now, you will be late.)

STORY READING INSTRUCTIONS
Students read pages pages 20–23 with the teacher.

COMPREHENSION PROCESSES
Remember, Understand, Apply, Analyze, Evaluate

PROCEDURES

1. Reviewing pages 18 and 19

**Summarizing; Locating Information; Describing;
Using Vocabulary—panic, destroy**

Have students turn to page 18. Quickly discuss the questions from the previous Setting a Purpose. Say something like:

You read pages 18 and 19 on your own. Let's see if you can answer the questions on the board. If we can't, what can we do? (We can look in our books.)

Why was the white blood cell chasing the bus? (It thought the bus was a germ.)

That's right. We know that white blood cells destroy germs. What do you think the white blood cell would try to do to the bus? (The white blood cell would try to destroy the bus.)

What did the kids hitch a ride on? (They hitched a ride on a red blood cell.)

Why did Arnold begin to panic? (He was lost.)

2. Introducing pages 20–23

Viewing, Predicting

Look at the picture on page 20. What do you think we are going to learn about next? (We'll learn about the heart . . .)

3. First Reading
- Ask questions and discuss the story as indicated by the blue text in this guide.
- Mix group and individual turns, independent of your voice.
  Have students work toward a group accuracy goal of 0–5 errors.
- After reading the story, practice any difficult words.
  Reread the story if students have not reached the accuracy goal.

4. Partner or Whisper Reading: Repeated Reading

 Before beginning independent work, have students finger track and partner or whisper read.

5. Comprehension and Skill Work
Tell students they will do Comprehension and Skill Activity 5 and work on The Human Body Entry 3 after they read pages 20–23. Guide practice, as needed. For teacher directions, see pages 66 and 67. Assign the Extra Fluency Passage, as appropriate.

6. Homework 4: New Passage

After Reading Page 20: Your Heart Is a Pump

❶ Apply: Inferring—Main Idea
What does Florrie's report explain?
(Florrie's report explains what the heart does.)

After Reading Page 20

❷ Understand: Explaining; Using Vocabulary—oxygen
What does the heart do?
(It pumps blood into the lungs.)
What happens in the lungs?
(The blood gets fresh oxygen.)

❸ Apply: Viewing; Inferring; Explaining
Look at the kids in the first chamber of the heart. Do you think they are having fun?
(No, they looked scared and upset.)

After Reading Page 21

❶ **Apply:** Inferring; Explaining; Using Vocabulary—panic
Why is Arnold's heart pounding?
(He is in a panic. He thinks he is lost.)

After Reading Page 22: Blood Goes Round and Round, One More Science Word

❶ Remember: Identifying—Fact
How long does it take your blood to go all through your body?
(It takes less than a minute.)

❷ Understand: Explaining—Fact; Using Vocabulary—circulate
Use the word *circulates* to explain what our blood does.
(Our blood circulates through the body.)

After Reading Page 22

❸ Analyze: Distinguishing Cause/Effect; **Apply:** Using Vocabulary—oxygen
What makes blood bright red?
(When the red blood cells go through the lungs, they pick up oxygen. The oxygen makes the red blood cells turn bright red.)

> **MODEL ENTHUSIASM**
>
> After completing the page, say something like:
> I'm really impressed with all that we are learning. I had no idea that our blood travels through our whole body in less than a minute!

After Reading Page 23

❶ **Apply:** Predicting
Where do you think the kids will go next?
(They'll go to the brain . . .)

❷ **Evaluate:** Responding; **Apply:** Explaining; Using Vocabulary—adventure
Would you rather be with Arnold or the kids? Why?
(I'd rather be with the kids. They're having a great adventure. I'd rather be with Arnold. I think traveling through a body would be yucky.)

PASSAGE READING FLUENCY

FLUENCY

Accuracy, Expression, Rate

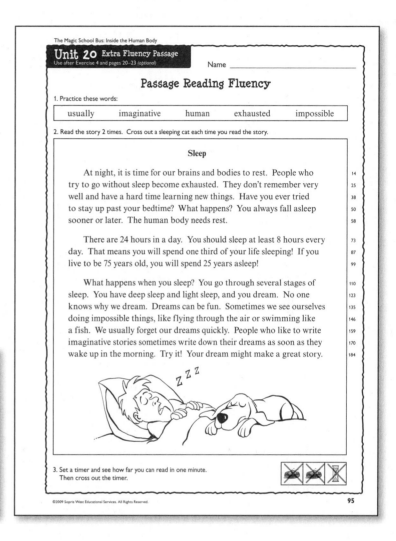

The Magic School Bus: Inside the Human Body

Unit 20 Extra Fluency Passage
Use after Exercise 4 and pages 20–23 *(optional)*

Name _____

Passage Reading Fluency

1. Practice these words:

| usually | imaginative | human | exhausted | impossible |

2. Read the story 2 times. Cross out a sleeping cat each time you read the story.

Sleep

At night, it is time for our brains and bodies to rest. People who try to go without sleep become exhausted. They don't remember very well and have a hard time learning new things. Have you ever tried to stay up past your bedtime? What happens? You always fall asleep sooner or later. The human body needs rest.

There are 24 hours in a day. You should sleep at least 8 hours every day. That means you will spend one third of your life sleeping! If you live to be 75 years old, you will spend 25 years asleep!

What happens when you sleep? You go through several stages of sleep. You have deep sleep and light sleep, and you dream. No one knows why we dream. Dreams can be fun. Sometimes we see ourselves doing impossible things, like flying through the air or swimming like a fish. We usually forget our dreams quickly. People who like to write imaginative stories sometimes write down their dreams as soon as they wake up in the morning. Try it! Your dream might make a great story.

14
25
38
50
58

73
87
99

110
123
135
146
159
170
184

3. Set a timer and see how far you can read in one minute. Then cross out the timer.

©2009 Sopris West Educational Services. All Rights Reserved.

95

ENHANCING PRACTICE WITH TEACHER-DIRECTED INSTRUCTION

If you are on the 8-Day Plan, you may wish to have students read the fluency passage out loud with you before students do independent Repeated Readings. Have students read the entire passage for accuracy. Then do Short Passage Practice.

• Model a paragraph.
• Have students read the paragraph with you.
• Have individuals read the paragraph.

Repeat with the next paragraphs.

PROCEDURES

For each step, demonstrate and guide practice, as needed. Then have students complete the page independently.

Passage Reading—Basic Instructions

• Have students read the practice words.
• Have students finger track and whisper read the story two times—the first time for accuracy and the second time for expression. Have students cross out a sleeping cat each time they finish.
• Have students do a one-minute Timed Reading and cross out the timer.

VOCABULARY AND ALPHABETICAL ORDER

COMPREHENSION PROCESSES
Understand, Apply

WRITING TRAITS
Conventions—Complete Sentence, Capital, Period
Presentation

Alphabetical Order

Defining and Using Vocabulary—experiment; Visualizing; Illustrating

Defining and Using Vocabulary—glimpse; Visualizing; Illustrating

Defining and Using Vocabulary—oxygen Visualizing, Illustrating

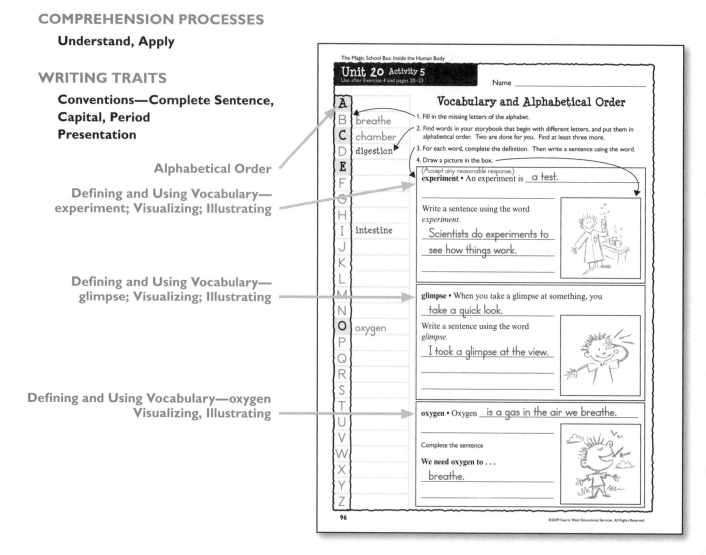

PROCEDURES
For each step, demonstrate and guide practice, as needed. Then have students complete the page independently.

Alphabetical Order—Basic Instructions
• Have students read the letters in the alphabet column and fill in the missing letters.
• Tell students they are going to find words in their storybook and write them in alphabetical order. Have students read the two examples given. Then have students select and write at least three more words from the storybook.

Vocabulary: Sentence Completion/Writing, Illustrating—Basic Instructions
• Have students read the vocabulary words.
• Have students complete the definitions by completing each sentence starter or filling in the blank.
• Have students complete or write a sentence using each vocabulary word. Visualize and illustrate, as appropriate.

ENTRY 3

COMPREHENSION PROCESSES
Understand, Apply

WRITING TRAITS
Conventions—Complete Sentence, Capital, Period

Using Graphic Organizer Viewing; Explaining—Fact Sentence Writing

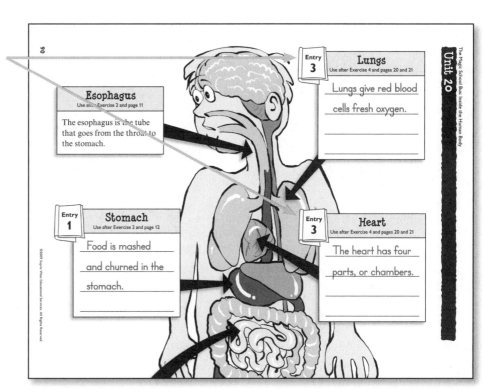

Esophagus
Use after Exercise 2 and page 11

The esophagus is the tube that goes from the throat to the stomach.

Lungs
Entry 3
Use after Exercise 4 and pages 20 and 21

Lungs give red blood cells fresh oxygen.

Stomach
Entry 1
Use after Exercise 2 and page 12

Food is mashed and churned in the stomach.

Heart
Entry 3
Use after Exercise 4 and pages 20 and 21

The heart has four parts, or chambers.

The Magic School Bus: Inside the Human Body
Unit 2o

PROCEDURES

Have students complete the page independently. Guide practice, only as needed.

Human Body: Diagram, Caption Writing—Specific Instructions
• Have students look at the diagram of the human body.
• Have students write a short caption about the lungs. Remind students that they can look at storybook pages 20 and 21 for information about the lungs.
• Have students write a short caption about the heart. Remind students that they can look at storybook pages 20 and 21 for information about the heart.
• Remind students to use a complete sentence, capitals, and a period.

1 SOUND REVIEW

2 SHIFTY WORD BLENDING

3 ACCURACY AND FLUENCY BUILDING

C1. Multisyllabic Words

- For the list of words divided by syllables, have students read each syllable, then the whole word. Use the word in a sentence, as appropriate.
- For the list of whole words, build accuracy, then fluency.

<table>
<tr><td>emerged</td><td>The butterfly came out or . . . emerged . . . from the cocoon.</td></tr>
<tr><td>contract</td><td>When muscles pull inward or get shorter, they . . . contract.</td></tr>
<tr><td>nasal</td><td>The inside of the nose is the . . . nasal . . . cavity.</td></tr>
<tr><td>functions</td><td>Different cells in the body have different . . . functions.</td></tr>
<tr><td>fiber</td><td>A strand of muscle is called a muscle . . . fiber.</td></tr>
<tr><td>cavity</td><td>A hollow space is called a . . . cavity.</td></tr>
<tr><td>deafening</td><td>The loud boom from the fireworks was . . . deafening.</td></tr>
<tr><td>constantly</td><td>My little sister never stops talking. She talks . . . constantly.</td></tr>
</table>

D1. Tricky Words

- For each Tricky Word, have students use the sounds and word parts they know to silently sound out the word. Use the word in a sentence to help with pronunciation.
- If the word is unfamiliar, tell students the word.

gesundheit

Look at the first word. The word is *gesundheit*. Read the word. (gesundheit)
When you sneeze, someone might say . . . *gesundheit*.
Read the word three times. (gesundheit, gesundheit, gesundheit)

receiving

Look at the next word. This is a tricky word, but I think you smart kids can sound it out. Thumbs up when you know the word. Use my sentence to help you. People like giving, but they also like . . . *receiving*. Read the word three times. (receiving, receiving, receiving)

bacteria

Look at the next word. Silently sound out the word. Then give me a thumbs-up. Now complete this sentence. You can get sick from . . . *bacteria*. Read the word three times. (bacteria, bacteria, bacteria)

lies	The dog . . . *lies* . . . next to the fireplace.
lose	The team played hard so they wouldn't . . . *lose*.

- Have students go back and read the whole words in the column.

4 WORD ENDINGS

5 WORDS IN CONTEXT

For each word, have students use the sounds and word parts they know to silently sound out the word. Then have students read the sentence. Assist, as needed.

6 MORPHOGRAPHS AND AFFIXES

> ACCURACY AND FLUENCY BUILDING (Reminder)
>
> For each task, have students say any underlined part, then read the word.
>
> Set a pace. Then have students read the whole words in each task and column.
>
> Provide repeated practice, building accuracy first, then fluency.

7 GENERALIZATION: READING NEW WORDS IN PARAGRAPHS

- Have students read the paragraph silently, then out loud. Tell students to use the sounds and word parts they know to read any difficult words.
- Repeat practice, as needed.

The Magic School Bus: Inside the Human Body

Unit 20 Exercise 5
Use before pages 24–31

1. SOUND REVIEW Use selected Sound Cards from Units 1–19.

2. SHIFTY WORD BLENDING For each word, have students say the underlined part, sound out smoothly, then read the word.

p<u>ai</u>n	<u>r</u>ain	<u>br</u>ain	brai<u>d</u>	br<u>ea</u>d

3. ACCURACY/FLUENCY BUILDING For each column, have students say any underlined part, then read each word. Next, have them read the column.

A1 Mixed Practice	**B1** Reading by Analogy	**C1** Multisyllabic Words		**D1** Tricky Words
<u>a</u>fraid	chief	e•merged	emerged	gesundheit
<u>A</u>manda	belief	con•tract	contract	receiving
n<u>er</u>ve	relief	na•sal	nasal	bacteria
for<u>ce</u>		func•tions	functions	lies
spee<u>ch</u>	Minnie	fi•ber	fiber	lose
fl<u>oa</u>ted	cookie	cav•i•ty	cavity	
m<u>o</u>tor	hankie	deaf•en•ing	deafening	
		con•stant•ly	constantly	

4. WORD ENDINGS Have students read any underlined word, then the word with an ending.

Ⓐ	<u>grossed</u>	<u>bundles</u>	<u>branched</u>	<u>stretching</u>
Ⓑ	tickle	tickling	pink	pinkish

5. WORDS IN CONTEXT Have students use the sounds and word parts they know to figure out each word. Then have them read each sentence.

Ⓐ	cer•e•bel•lum	The <u>cerebellum</u> is the part of the brain that controls our muscles and helps us balance.
Ⓑ	spi•nal cord	The <u>spinal cord</u> is the band of nerves that stretch from the brain down the center of the backbone.
Ⓒ	ce•re•bral cor•tex	The <u>cerebral cortex</u> is the outer surface of the brain.

6. MORPHOGRAPHS AND AFFIXES Have students read the underlined part, then the word.

<u>pre</u>pare	<u>re</u>main	<u>vis</u>ion	tremend<u>ous</u>	power<u>ful</u>

7. GENERALIZATION Have students read the paragraph silently, then out loud. (New words: Phoebe, Arnold, heartbeat)

Phoebe and Arnold were late for school. They ran from the bus stop to her classroom. When they arrived at class, Phoebe said, "Wow, my heartbeat is faster than usual. I am sure it is because I was running and using energy."

73

MASTERY TEACHING/ DISCRIMINATION PRACTICE

Repeated Practice

Provide repeated practice on each task. If you hear an error, gently correct the whole group with a demonstration and/or guided practice. Move to another skill or task, then return to the difficult item many times—mixing group and individual turns, independent of your voice. When a task is easy, build speed of recognition.

Remember, practice makes perfect! And practice builds fluency.

COMPREHENSION PROCESSES

Apply

PROCEDURES

Introducing Vocabulary

> ★**function** ★**control** ★**constantly** ★**lose my nerve** ★**relief** ★**emerge**

- For each vocabulary word, have students read the word by parts, then read the whole word.
- Read the student-friendly explanations to students as they follow with their fingers. Then have students use the vocabulary word by following the gray text.
- Review and discuss the illustrations.
  Note: Student vocabulary pages for this unit are found in the students' *Exercise Book 3*.

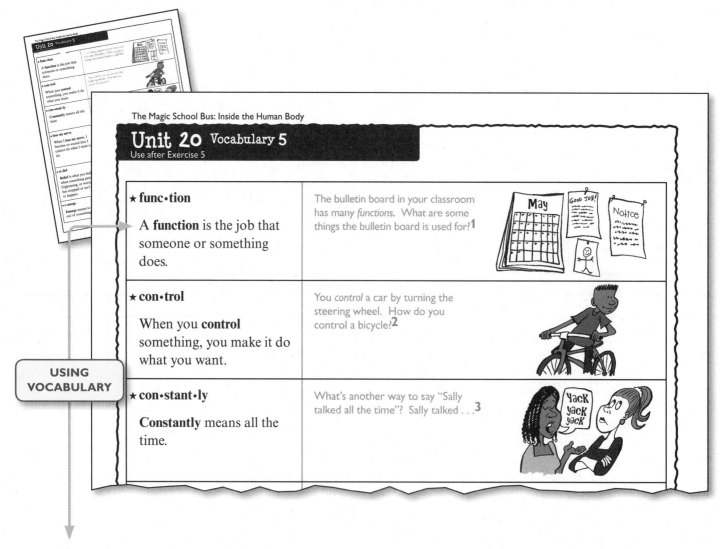

The Magic School Bus: Inside the Human Body

Unit 20 Vocabulary 5
Use after Exercise 5

★ **func•tion** A **function** is the job that someone or something does.	The bulletin board in your classroom has many *functions*. What are some things the bulletin board is used for?**1**
★ **con•trol** When you **control** something, you make it do what you want.	You *control* a car by turning the steering wheel. How do you control a bicycle?**2**
★ **con•stant•ly** **Constantly** means all the time.	What's another way to say "Sally talked all the time"? Sally talked . . .**3**

USING VOCABULARY

❶ **Apply:** Using Vocabulary—function (The bulletin board is for putting up events and pictures to share.)

❷ **Apply:** Using Vocabulary—control (You control a bicycle by turning the handlebars.)

❸ **Apply:** Using Vocabulary—constantly (constantly)

★ = New in this unit

USING VOCABULARY

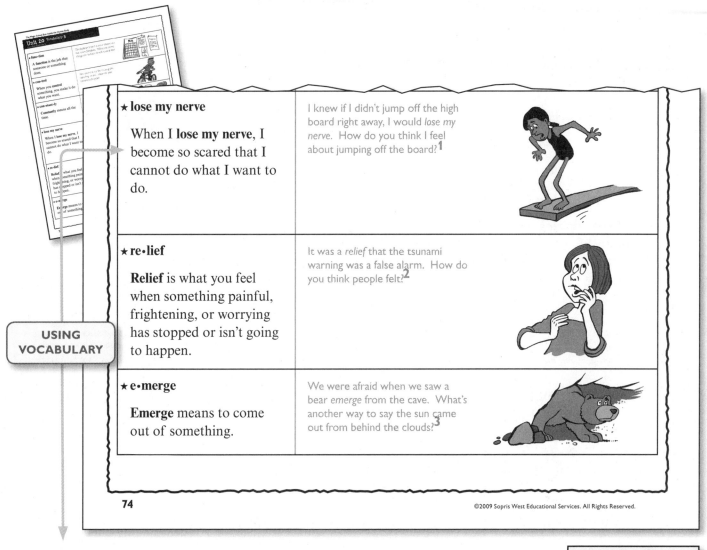

★ **lose my nerve**

When I **lose my nerve**, I become so scared that I cannot do what I want to do.

I knew if I didn't jump off the high board right away, I would *lose my nerve*. How do you think I feel about jumping off the board?[1]

★ **re•lief**

Relief is what you feel when something painful, frightening, or worrying has stopped or isn't going to happen.

It was a *relief* that the tsunami warning was a false alarm. How do you think people felt?[2]

★ **e•merge**

Emerge means to come out of something.

We were afraid when we saw a bear *emerge* from the cave. What's another way to say the sun came out from behind the clouds?[3]

74

❶ **Apply:** Using Idioms and Expressions—lose my nerve (I feel scared.)

❷ **Apply:** Using Vocabulary—relief, false alarm (People felt happy. They could stop worrying about the tsunami.)

❸ **Apply:** Using Vocabulary—emerge (The sun emerged from behind the clouds.)

USING VOCABULARY

Be enthusiastic about learning new words. Keep a running list of words you would like to use and encourage students to use. Keep the list handy when you are teaching. Put students' names on the board to acknowledge use of a word. Say things like:

Wow! [Rachel] used the word *relief* when she found out the storm was over.

STORY READING INSTRUCTIONS

Students read pages 24–27 with the teacher and pages 28–31 on
their own.

Note: If you're working on an 8-Day Plan, you will read pages 28–31
with students.

COMPREHENSION PROCESSES

Understand, Apply, Analyze

PROCEDURES

1. Reviewing pages 20–23

Summarizing, Describing

Quickly discuss what has happened in the story so far. Say something like:

This book has two stories in it. One story is about Ms. Frizzle's class.

So far, the kids in Ms. Frizzle's class have had quite an adventure!

How would you describe their journey?

(It's been amazing, fascinating, absurd . . .)

The other story is about Arnold. Why is Arnold's story separate?

(He got left behind. The bus is in his body. He was lost.)

> **CORRECTING DECODING ERRORS**
>
> During story reading, gently correct any error, then have students reread the sentence.

2. Introducing pages 24–27

Say something like:

This part is about the brain. That should be interesting.

Listen for interesting facts that you can tell your parents.

They will be impressed with what you know.

3. First Reading

- Ask questions and discuss the story as indicated by the blue text in
  this guide.
- Mix group and individual turns, independent of your voice.
  Have students work toward a group accuracy goal of 0–6 errors.
  Quietly keep track of errors made by all students in the group.
- After reading the story, practice any difficult words.
  Reread the story if students have not reached the accuracy goal.

4. Second Reading, Short Passage Practice: Developing Prosody

- Demonstrate expressive, fluent reading of the first paragraph.
  Read at a rate slightly faster than the students' rate.
- Guide practice with your voice.
- Provide individual turns while others track with their fingers and
  whisper read.
- Repeat with one paragraph at a time.

After Reading Page 24: Your Brain Is Always Working

❶ Understand: Explaining—Fact; Using Vocabulary—control
What does the brain control?
(The brain controls heartbeat, breathing, and other body functions.)

❷ Apply: Inferring, Explaining
Why does Alex say, "Your brain never lies down on the job"?
(The brain is at work, even when you're sleeping.)

After Reading Page 24

❸ Apply: Inferring; Explaining; Using Vocabulary—senses, control
Why is the cerebral cortex important?
(The cerebral cortex controls our senses—seeing, hearing, smelling, touching, and tasting. It also controls talking, moving, and thinking.)

After Reading Page 25

❶ **Apply:** Inferring, Explaining
What are the kids doing now?
(The kids are walking on the brain.)

❷ **Analyze:** Inferring; Distinguishing Cause/Effect
If someone has trouble with their balance, what part of the brain might be having problems?
(The cerebellum helps you keep your balance, so maybe there is trouble with the cerebellum.)

After Reading Page 25: Arnold's Thought Bubble

❸ **Apply:** Inferring, Explaining
What is Arnold doing now?
(He is thinking. He is thinking about how to get back to school.)

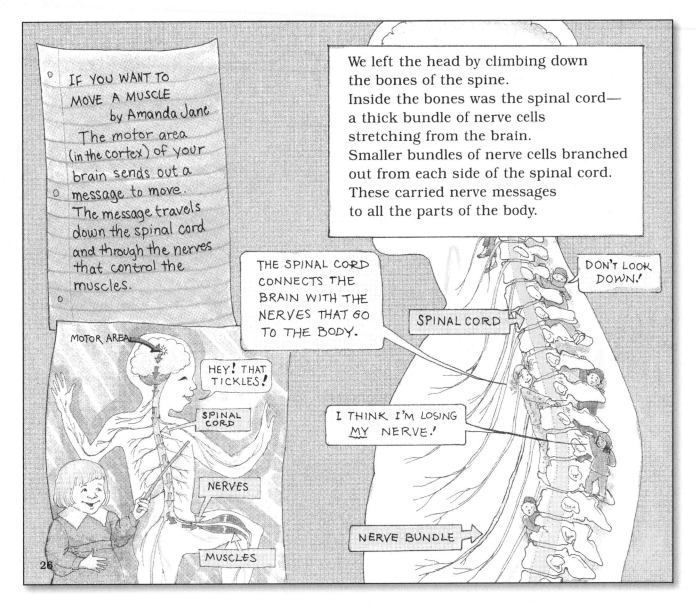

After Reading Page 26

❶ Understand: Explaining
Look at the picture. What are the kids doing now?
(They're climbing down the spine.)

❷ Apply: Inferring
What's another word for spine?
(The spine is the backbone.)

❸ Apply: Explaining
What is the spinal cord, and what does it do?
(The spinal cord is a big bundle of nerve cells stretching from the brain. The spinal cord carries messages from the brain to all parts of the body.)

After Reading Page 27: Left Panel

❶ **Understand:** Viewing, Explaining
Look at the picture. What are the kids doing now?
(They're sliding down the muscles.)

After Reading Page 27

❷ **Understand:** Explaining, Inferring
What is Arnold doing?
(He's running back to school.)

❸ **Apply:** Explaining, Inferring
Why is Arnold's heart beating faster?
(He's running. The more active you are, the faster your heart beats.)

STORY READING INSTRUCTIONS

Students read pages 28–31 without the teacher, independently or with partners.

Note: If you're working on an 8-Day Plan, you will read pages 28–31 with students.

COMPREHENSION PROCESSES

Understand, Apply

PROCEDURES

1. Getting Ready

Have students turn to page 28.

2. Setting a Purpose

Explaining, Inferring

Before you begin reading, say something like:

Read to find out the answers to these questions:
- Where did the kids end up?
- What makes you sneeze?
- How do you think the school bus is going to get out of Arnold's body?

3. Reading on Your Own: Partner or Whisper Reading

- Have students take turns reading every other page with a partner or have students whisper read pages 28–31 on their own.
- Continue having students track each word with their fingers.

4. Comprehension and Skill Work

For students on a 6-Day Plan, tell students that they will do Comprehension and Skill Activity 6 and work on The Human Body Entry 4 after they read on their own. Guide practice, as needed. For teacher directions, see pages 82 and 84. (For 8-Day Plans, see the Lesson Planner, page 9.)

5. Homework 5: New Passage

When we emerged from the bloodsteam,
we were in a huge open space.
"Where are we?" asked a kid.
Ms. Frizzle explained,
"Children, this is the nasal cavity."
"The what?" we asked.
"The inside of the nose," said The Friz.
Suddenly, we heard a deafening noise.
It sounded like "Ah-aa-aa-ah!"

WE'RE IN A NOSE?

THIS TIME SHE'S GONE TOO FAR.

I AM SO GROSSED OUT!

I THINK I'M GOING TO SNEEZE...

USE YOUR HANKIE.

29

STORY COMPREHENSION • CAUSE AND EFFECT

COMPREHENSION PROCESSES
Remember, Understand

PROCEDURES
For each step, demonstrate and guide practice, as needed. Then have students complete the page independently.

Cause/Effect: Sequence Chart—Specific Instructions
Have students identify the cause and effect events by reading the boxes and completing the sentences with words from the word bank. Have students cross out a word as it is used.

Self-monitoring
Have students check and correct their work.

Using Graphic
Organizer
Identifying—
What, Sentence
Completion
Using Vocabulary—
esophagus, panic

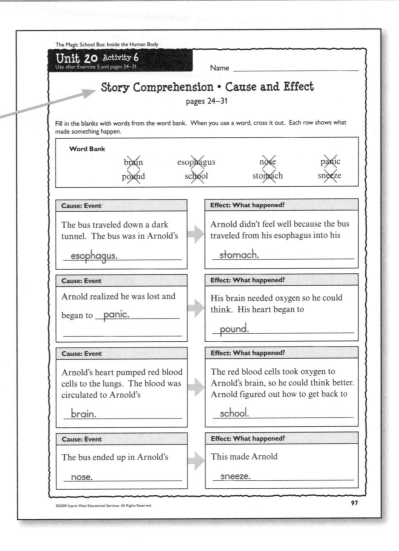

The Magic School Bus: Inside the Human Body

Unit 20 Activity 6
Use after Exercise 5 and pages 24–31

Name _____

Story Comprehension • Cause and Effect
pages 24–31

Fill in the blanks with words from the word bank. When you use a word, cross it out. Each row shows what made something happen.

Word Bank

~~brain~~   ~~esophagus~~   ~~nose~~   ~~panic~~
~~pound~~   ~~school~~   ~~stomach~~   ~~sneeze~~

Cause: Event	Effect: What happened?
The bus traveled down a dark tunnel. The bus was in Arnold's _esophagus._	Arnold didn't feel well because the bus traveled from his esophagus into his _stomach._
Arnold realized he was lost and began to _panic._	His brain needed oxygen so he could think. His heart began to _pound._
Arnold's heart pumped red blood cells to the lungs. The blood was circulated to Arnold's _brain._	The red blood cells took oxygen to Arnold's brain, so he could think better. Arnold figured out how to get back to _school._
The bus ended up in Arnold's _nose._	This made Arnold _sneeze._

©2009 Sopris West Educational Services. All Rights Reserved.

97

83

ENTRY 4

COMPREHENSION PROCESSES

Understand, Apply

WRITING TRAITS

Conventions—Complete Sentence, Capital, Period

Using Graphic Organizer; Viewing Explaining—Fact; Sentence Writing

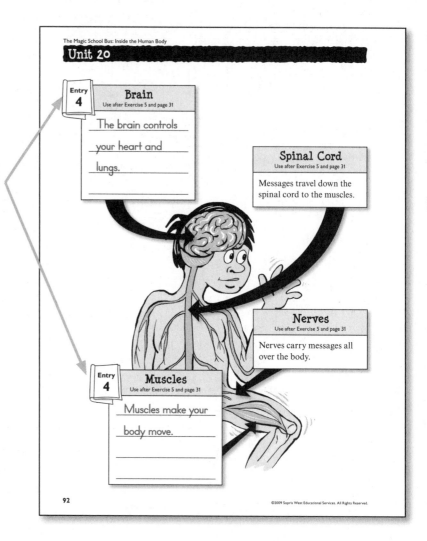

The Magic School Bus: Inside the Human Body

Unit 20

| Entry 4 | **Brain** |
| Use after Exercise 5 and page 31 |

The brain controls your heart and lungs.

Spinal Cord
Use after Exercise 5 and page 31

Messages travel down the spinal cord to the muscles.

Nerves
Use after Exercise 5 and page 31

Nerves carry messages all over the body.

| Entry 4 | **Muscles** |
| Use after Exercise 5 and page 31 |

Muscles make your body move.

92 ©2009 Sopris West Educational Services. All Rights Reserved.

PROCEDURES

Have students complete the page independently. Guide practice, only as needed.

Human Body: Diagram, Caption Writing—Specific Instructions
- Have students look at the diagram of the human body.
- Have students write a short caption about the brain. Remind students that they can look at storybook page 24 and 25 for information about the brain.
- Have students read the caption about the spinal cord and nerves.
- Have students write a short caption about the muscles. Remind students that they can look at storybook pages 26 and 27 for information about the muscles.
- Remind them to use a complete sentence, capitals, and a period.

JUST FOR FUN • MY FAVORITE ORGAN

HOW TO USE "JUST FOR FUN" ACTIVITIES

Note: This activity is optional and is *just for fun.* Use the activity:

- as a cushion activity
- for homework
- just for fun

PROCEDURES

As time allows, have students choose an organ, then illustrate and write two sentences about it. Then have them write a speech balloon caption for the bird. This page may be given to students as homework.

❶ SOUND REVIEW

❷ SHIFTY WORD BLENDING

❸ ACCURACY AND FLUENCY BUILDING
- For each task, have students say any underlined part, then read the word.
- Set a pace. Then have students read the whole words in each task and column.
- Provide repeated practice, building accuracy first, then fluency.

B1. Reading by Analogy
>   Have students figure out how to read -*ney* by reading other words they know.

C1. Multisyllabic Words
- For the list of words divided by syllables, have students read each syllable, then the whole word. Use the word in a sentence, as appropriate.
- For the list of whole words, build accuracy and then fluency.

enlarged	When something is larger than it should be, it is . . . *enlarged*.
capture	The police chased the thieves for miles but could not . . . *capture* . . . them.
esophagus	We swallow food by using muscles in the . . . *esophagus*.
microscope	Amy looked at the very small bug through a . . . *microscope*.
intestine	Food goes from the stomach to the small . . . *intestine*.
bladder	The part of the body that holds liquid waste is the . . . *bladder*.
vessel	Blood flows through a tube called a blood . . . *vessel*.
bulletin	Our class picture was posted on the . . . *bulletin* . . . board.

D1. Tricky Words
- For each Tricky Word, have students use the sounds and word parts they know to silently sound out the word. Use the word in a sentence to help with pronunciation.
- If the word is unfamiliar, tell students the word.

system
Look at the first word. The word is *system*. Say the word. (system) Blood is part of the circulatory . . . *system*. Read the word three times. (system, system, system)

tour
Look at the next word. Silently sound out the word and give me a thumbs-up when you know it. Use my sentence to help you. We went on a bus . . . *tour*.
Read the word three times. (tour, tour, tour)

tissue
Look at the next word. I think you can sound out this word. Thumbs up when you know the word. Read the word. (tissue) People all have skin . . . *tissue*.
Read the word three times. (tissue, tissue, tissue)

false	The answer was either true or . . . *false*.
weird	That costume looks really strange or . . . *weird*.
ideas	Have you got any new . . . *ideas*?
course	Arnold wanted to go, too, of . . . *course*.

- Have students go back and read the whole words in the column.

❹ WORDS IN CONTEXT

⑤ MORPHOGRAPHS AND AFFIXES
- Have students read the underlined part, then the word.
- Repeat practice with whole words, building accuracy, then fluency.

⑥ GENERALIZATION: READING NEW WORDS IN PARAGRAPHS

The Magic School Bus: Inside the Human Body

Unit 20 Exercise 6
Use before pages 32–37

1. SOUND REVIEW Use selected Sound Cards from Units 1–19.

2. SHIFTY WORD BLENDING For each word, have students say the underlined part, sound out smoothly, then read the word.

| sp<u>i</u>ne | sp<u>i</u>te | <u>bi</u>te | b<u>i</u>le | <u>whi</u>le |

3. ACCURACY/FLUENCY BUILDING For each column, have students say any underlined part, then read each word. Next, have them read the column.

A1 Mixed Practice	**B1** Reading by Analogy	**C1** Multisyllabic Words		**D1** Tricky Words
g<u>er</u>ms	honey	en·larged	enlarged	system
liv<u>er</u>	money	cap·ture	capture	tour
b<u>oar</u>d	kidney	e·soph·a·gus	esophagus	tissue
dr<u>aw</u>	**B2** Compound Words	mi·cro·scope	microscope	false
p<u>oi</u>sons		in·tes·tine	intestine	weird
destr<u>oy</u>s	otherwise	blad·der	bladder	ideas
ent<u>er</u>	windpipe	ves·sel	vessel	course
s<u>o</u>lar	gallbladder	bul·le·tin	bulletin	

4. WORDS IN CONTEXT Have students use the sounds and word parts they know to figure out each word. Then have them read each sentence.

| Ⓐ ur·ine | <u>Urine</u> is liquid waste from the body. |
| Ⓑ vi·ta·mins | Fruits and vegetables have lots of <u>vitamins</u>. |

5. MORPHOGRAPHS AND AFFIXES Have students read the underlined part, then the word.

| great<u>ly</u> | believ<u>able</u> | <u>un</u>believable | <u>be</u>have | good<u>ness</u> |

6. GENERALIZATION Have students read the paragraph silently, then out loud. (New words: author, organs, video)

Yesterday, Mrs. Lopez, the author of the book *Your Organs and You: How to Stay Healthy*, came to visit our class. She gave us information about how all the different organs in our bodies work. She even brought models of organs. Our teacher took a video of the whole thing. At the end of the talk, all the kids surrounded her so they could ask questions.

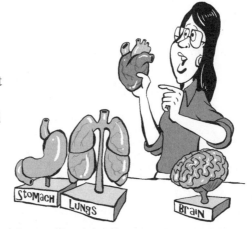

75

COMPREHENSION PROCESSES

Understand, Apply

PROCEDURES

1. Introducing Vocabulary

☆ business as usual ☆ organ, function, constantly

• For each vocabulary word, have students read the word by parts, then read the whole word.
• Read the student-friendly explanations to students as they follow with their fingers. Then have students use the vocabulary word by following the gray text.
• Review and discuss the illustrations.
  Note: Student vocabulary pages for this unit are found in the students' *Exercise Book 3*.

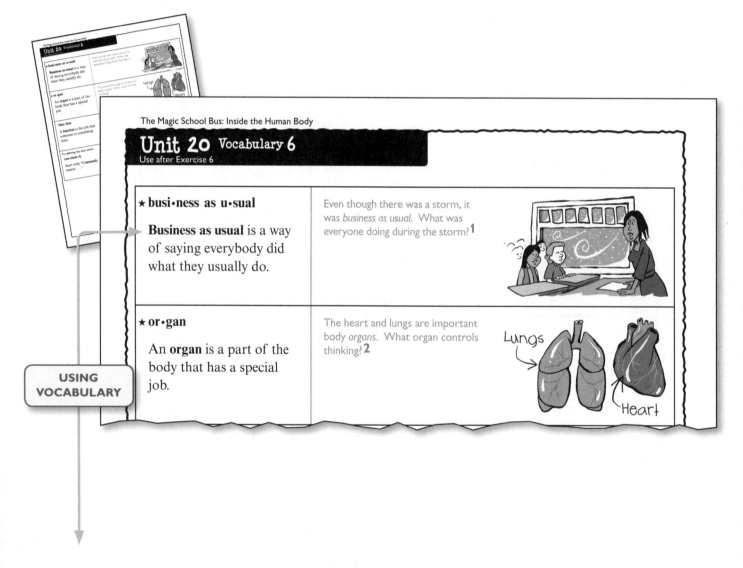

USING
VOCABULARY

The Magic School Bus: Inside the Human Body

Unit 20 Vocabulary 6
Use after Exercise 6

★ busi•ness as u•sual

Business as usual is a way of saying everybody did what they usually do.

Even though there was a storm, it was *business as usual*. What was everyone doing during the storm?**1**

★ or•gan

An **organ** is a part of the body that has a special job.

The heart and lungs are important body *organs*. What organ controls thinking?**2**

Lungs

Heart

❶ **Apply:** Using Idioms and Expressions—business as usual (Everyone was doing what they usually do.)
❷ **Apply:** Using Vocabulary—organ (The brain controls thinking.)

☆ = New in this unit

2. Now You Try It!
- Have students read the last word by parts and then read the whole word.
- Have students explain or define the word in their own words, then use the word in a sentence.

USING VOCABULARY

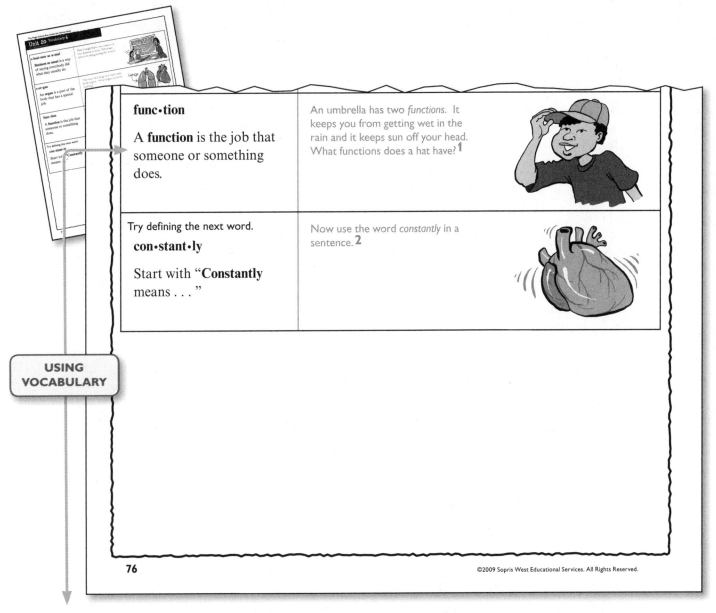

func•tion

A **function** is the job that someone or something does.

An umbrella has two *functions*. It keeps you from getting wet in the rain and it keeps sun off your head. What functions does a hat have?**1**

Try defining the next word.
con•stant•ly

Start with "**Constantly** means . . ."

Now use the word *constantly* in a sentence.**2**

76　　　　　　　　　　©2009 Sopris West Educational Services. All Rights Reserved.

❶ **Apply:** Using Vocabulary—function (A hat's functions are to keep your head dry and warm. A hat keeps sun off your head too. A hat can also make you look cool . . .)

❷ **Understand:** Defining and Using Vocabulary—constantly (Constantly means all the time. I like to chew gum constantly.)

STORY READING INSTRUCTIONS
Students read pages 32–37 with the teacher.

COMPREHENSION PROCESSES
Understand, Apply, Evaluate

PROCEDURES

1. **Reviewing pages 28–31**

   Summarizing, Inferring

   Have students turn to page 28. Quickly discuss questions from the previous Setting a Purpose. Say something like:

   Yesterday you read pages 28–31 on your own. Can you answer these questions now?

   Where did the kids end up? (They ended up in Arnold's nose.)

   What makes you sneeze? (Your brain feels the tickling in your nose. Your brain makes you take a breath. Then your brain makes your chest muscles squeeze your lungs, and air rushes out your nose. That's when you sneeze.)

   How do you think the school bus is going to get out of Arnold's body?

   (Arnold is going to sneeze.)

2. **Introducing pages 32–37**

   Predicting

   Say something like:

   We're going to finish the book today. How do you think it will end? (The kids will get out of Arnold's body and tell him all about the ride . . .)

3. **First Reading**
   - Ask questions and discuss the story as indicated by the blue text in this guide.
   - Mix group and individual turns, independent of your voice.
     Have students work toward a group accuracy goal of 0–4 errors.
     Quietly keep track of errors made by all students in the group.
   - After reading the story, practice any difficult words.
     Reread the story if students have not reached the accuracy goal.

4. **Second Reading, Timed Readings: Repeated Reading**

   - As time allows, have students do Timed Readings while others follow along.
   - Time individuals for 30 seconds and encourage each child to work for a personal best.
   - Determine words correct per minute. Record student scores.

5. **Partner or Whisper Reading: Repeated Reading**

   Before beginning independent work, have students finger track and partner or whisper read.

6. **Written Assessment (Comprehension and Skill)**

   Tell students they will do a Written Assessment after they read pages 32–37. (For teacher directions, see pages 97–99.)

7. **Homework 6: New Passage**

Before Reading Page 32

❶ Apply: Viewing, Inferring
There were two stories in this book. There was Arnold's story and another story about Ms. Frizzle's class. Look at pages 32 and 33. What do you think is happening now?
(Arnold and the class all get back together.)

After Reading Page 33

❶ **Apply:** Inferring, Explaining
How do the kids feel about Arnold? How can you tell?
(The kids like Arnold. They are glad to see him. They were worried about him.)

THE KIDNEYS CLEAN YOUR BLOOD AND MAKE URINE.

THE BLADDER STORES URINE.

KIDNEYS

BLADDER

LIVER

STOMACH

THE LIVER STORES VITAMINS AND DESTROYS POISONS. IT ALSO MAKES BILE, A FLUID THAT HELPS DIGEST FATTY FOODS.

Back in the classroom, it was business as usual. Ms. Frizzle made us draw a chart of the human body for the bulletin board.

NERVE

BLOOD VESSEL

BONE

MUSCLE

34

After Reading Page 34

❶ **Apply:** Inferring; Explaining; Using Idioms and Expressions—business as usual
Why does the book say "it was business as usual"?
(The kids are back in the classroom, doing what they usually do.)

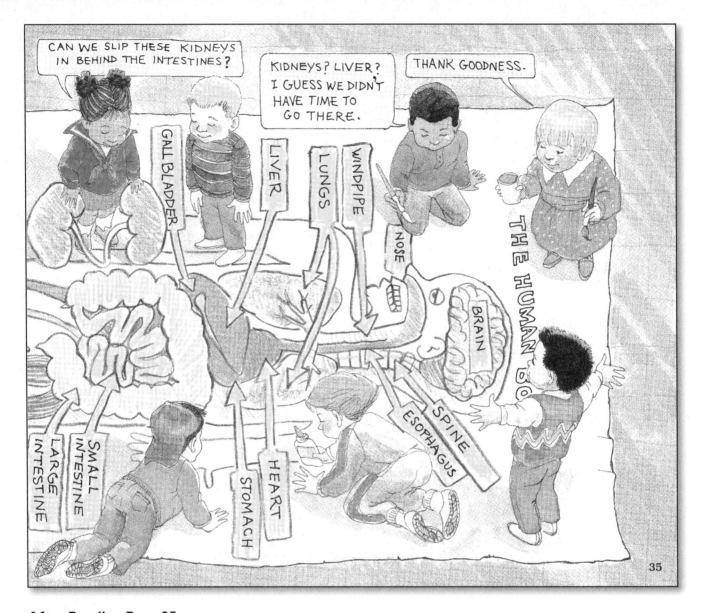

After Reading Page 35

1 Understand: Describing
Describe what the kids are doing.
(They are making a huge chart of the human body. They are drawing and labeling the body parts.)

After Reading Page 36

1 **Evaluate:** Responding; **Apply:** Using Vocabulary—fascinate
One of the kids says she would rather go to Hawaii than take another trip through the human body. Would you rather go to Hawaii or take a ride through the human body? Why?
(I would rather take a ride through the human body. It would be fascinating. I would rather go to Hawaii. It seems safer and nicer . . .)

After Reading Page 37

❶ Apply: Predicting
What do you think the class is going to study next?
(They are going to study space.)

❷ Evaluate: Responding
Would you want to go on a Magic School Bus adventure into space? Why or why not?
(I would like to go into space. It would be like being an astronaut. It wouldn't be as gross as traveling through Arnold's body . . .)

Note: If time allows, you may wish to take the test with students on pages 38 and 39 of *The Magic School Bus: Inside the Human Body.*
Have fun celebrating all your students have learned.

WRITTEN ASSESSMENT (1 of 3)

COMPREHENSION PROCESSES
Remember, Understand, Apply

WRITING TRAITS
Ideas and Content
Conventions—Complete Sentence, Capital, Period
Presentation

Test Taking ———➤

Unit 20 Written Assessment
Use after Exercise 6 and The Magic School Bus, pp 32–37

WARM-UP

control	messages	communicates	siren

The Amazing Brain

Your brain looks like a blob of chewed bubble gum. It is pink and covered with cracks. Even though it doesn't look important, it is the control center of your body.

The brain controls thinking. It even controls your heartbeat and breathing. Your brain is in charge of everything you do.

Your brain communicates with every part of your body. It sends messages that travel through the nerves. The nerves carry the messages out of the brain to your organs and muscles. The nerves also send messages back to your brain.

For example, when you hear a siren, the nerves in your ears send a message to your brain. "Listen to the loud noise." When you see the fire engine, the nerves in your eyes send a message to your brain. "Hey, look at the red truck." You recognize what you see and hear. It's a fire engine!

Your brain never stops working. It never stops to rest, not even when you are sleeping. A brain isn't just a blob. It's an amazing control center!

continued ➤

128

WRITTEN ASSESSMENT (2 of 3)

Identifying—Topic

Using Graphic Organizer (Chart)
Identifying—Supporting Details, Facts

Using Graphic Organizer (Chart)
Inferring—Main Idea; Sentence Writing
Using Vocabulary—control

Identifying—Fact

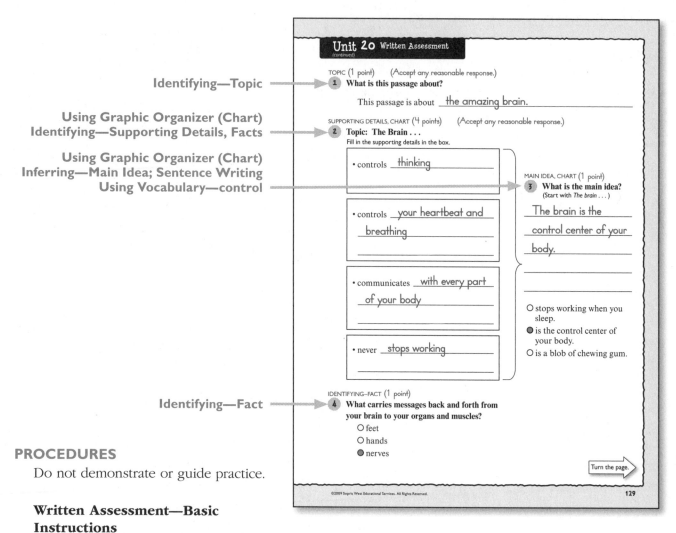

Unit 20 Written Assessment
(continued)

TOPIC (1 point)   (Accept any reasonable response.)
1 **What is this passage about?**

This passage is about ___the amazing brain.___

SUPPORTING DETAILS, CHART (4 points)   (Accept any reasonable response.)
2 **Topic: The Brain . . .**
Fill in the supporting details in the box.

• controls ___thinking___

• controls ___your heartbeat and breathing___

• communicates ___with every part of your body___

• never ___stops working___

MAIN IDEA, CHART (1 point)
3 **What is the main idea?**
(Start with *The brain . . .*)

___The brain is the control center of your body.___

○ stops working when you sleep.
● is the control center of your body.
○ is a blob of chewing gum.

IDENTIFYING–FACT (1 point)
4 **What carries messages back and forth from your brain to your organs and muscles?**
○ feet
○ hands
● nerves

Turn the page.

129

PROCEDURES

Do not demonstrate or guide practice.

Written Assessment—Basic Instructions

1. Introduce the Written Assessment.
   - Tell students that their work today is an opportunity for them to show what they can do independently. Say something like:

     You should be very proud of your accomplishments. Remember, on a Written Assessment, you get to show me what you can do all by yourself.

   - Tell students they will whisper read the passage and then answer the questions without help.

2. Check for student understanding.
   Say something like:

   Look at your assessment. What are you going to do first? (write my name)

   What are going to do next? (whisper read the passage)

   What will you do after you read the passage? (answer the questions)

   That's great. Now what will you do if you get to a hard question?
   (reread the question sind try again)

   That's right. What should you do if it's still hard? (reread the passage and try again)

   Very good. And if you still aren't sure, what will you do? (do my best and keep going)

WRITTEN ASSESSMENT (3 of 3)

Defining and Using Vocabulary—control

Drawing Conclusions; Explaining—Facts
Sentence Writing; Paragraph Writing

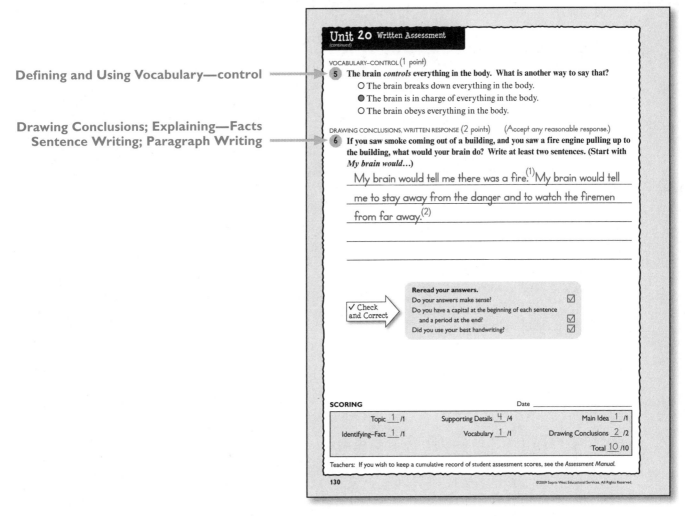

Unit 20 Written Assessment
(continued)

VOCABULARY–CONTROL (1 point)

5 The brain *controls* everything in the body. What is another way to say that?
○ The brain breaks down everything in the body.
● The brain is in charge of everything in the body.
○ The brain obeys everything in the body.

DRAWING CONCLUSIONS, WRITTEN RESPONSE (2 points)   (Accept any reasonable response.)

6 If you saw smoke coming out of a building, and you saw a fire engine pulling up to the building, what would your brain do? Write at least two sentences. (Start with *My brain would…*)

My brain would tell me there was a fire.(1) My brain would tell me to stay away from the danger and to watch the firemen from far away.(2)

✓ Check and Correct

Reread your answers.
Do your answers make sense? ☑
Do you have a capital at the beginning of each sentence and a period at the end? ☑
Did you use your best handwriting? ☑

SCORING   Date _____

Topic _1_ /1	Supporting Details _4_ /4	Main Idea _1_ /1
Identifying–Fact _1_ /1	Vocabulary _1_ /1	Drawing Conclusions _2_ /2
		Total _10_ /10

Teachers: If you wish to keep a cumulative record of student assessment scores, see the *Assessment Manual.*

130   ©2009 Sopris West Educational Services. All Rights Reserved.

3. Remind students to check and correct.
   When you finish your assessment, what should you do? (check and correct)
   That's right. Go to the top of the page. Reread the questions and make sure your answers make sense. Fix anything that doesn't sound right. Make sure you have an answer for every question.

4. Remind students what to do when they finish their work.

End of the Unit

In this section, you will find:

Making Decisions

As you near the end of the unit, plan to give the Written Assessment and the Oral Reading Fluency Assessment to each child in your group. Use this section as a general guide for making instructional decisions and doing diagnostic planning.

Written Assessment

The Unit 20 Written Assessment is located on page 127 of *Activity Book 3* and on the CD.

Oral Reading Fluency Assessment

The Unit 20 Oral Reading Fluency Assessment is located on page 104 of this teacher's guide and in the *Assessment Manual*.

Certificate of Achievement

Celebrate your children's accomplishments. When your students master the unit skills, send home the Certificate of Achievement.

Making Decisions

GENERAL ASSESSMENT GUIDELINES

1. After students read Story Reading 6, pages 32–37, give the group the Unit 20 Written Assessment in place of Comprehension and Skill Work. Follow the instructions on pages 97–99 of this guide.

2. While the group is completing the Written Assessment, or any time during the day, administer the Oral Reading Fluency Assessment. Assess each student individually.

   Optional: Graph the results of the assessment. (See Unit 7 Teacher's Guide, pages 92 and 95.)
   - If the student's words correct per minute go up, congratulate the student.
   - If the student's words correct per minute go down, discuss the student's overall improvement and help him or her identify ways to improve for the next assessment.

3. Score oral fluency responses on the Student Assessment Record. Adhere to the scoring criteria in the *Assessment Manual*. Use a stopwatch to time how long it takes each student to read the Oral Reading Fluency Passage, and record errors.

USING WRITTEN ASSESSMENT RESULTS

Results of the Written Assessment *should not* be used to determine whether a student or group of students continues forward in the program. As long as students pass the Oral Reading Fluency Assessment, they should continue forward with the next unit.

The Written Assessment should be used to informally monitor how well students read independently and answer questions in writing. If any student has difficulty with the Written Assessment, re-administer the assessment orally.

If the student has difficulty answering the questions orally:
- Record the types of errors (e.g., main idea, sequencing, open-ended response).
- Provide explicit instruction for these types of questions during reading group, before independent work, and in tutorials, as needed.
  1) Demonstrate (or model) appropriate responses, guide practice, and provide opportunities for independent practice.
  2) For inferential questions, think aloud with students—explain how you arrive at an answer.
  3) For literal questions, teach students to reread a passage, locate information, reread the question, and respond.

USING THE ORAL READING FLUENCY RESULTS

At the end of each unit, you will need to make decisions regarding student progress. Should students go forward in the program? Does the group need added decoding and fluency practice before proceeding? Do individuals require more assistance and practice to continue working in their group? These decisions all require use of the oral reading fluency data and professional judgment. As you analyze assessment results, watch for trends and anomalies.

See the *Assessment Manual* for detailed information and instructional recommendations. General guidelines and recommendations follow:

Strong Pass ≥ 123 WCPM 0–2 errors	• Continue with the current pace of instruction. • Have students set goals. (Until students are reading approximately 180 words correct per minute, oral reading fluency continues to be an instructional goal.)
Pass 102–122 WCPM 0–2 errors	• Continue with the current pace of instruction. Consider increasing fluency practice.
No Pass ≤ 101 WCPM	• If a child scores a No Pass but has previously passed all assessments, you may wish to advance the student to the next unit, then carefully monitor the student. • If a child scores a No Pass but has previously passed all assessments, you may wish to advance the student to the next unit and also provide additional practice opportunities. (See below.) • If a child scores two consecutive No Passes or periodic No Passes, additional practice must be provided. (See below.) • If a child scores three consecutive No Passes, the student should be placed in a lower-performing group.

RED FLAG
A No Pass is a red flag. A mild early intervention can prevent an intense and time-consuming intervention in the future.

Added Practice Options for Groups

Warm-Ups:
- Begin each lesson with Partner Reading of the previous day's homework.
- Begin each lesson with a five-minute Fluency Booster. Place copies of the Unit 15–19 *Read Well* Homework in three-ring notebooks. Each day, have students begin Finger Tracking and Whisper Reading at Unit 15, Homework 1. At the end of five minutes, have students mark where they are in their notebooks. The next day, the goal is to read farther.
- Begin each Story Reading with a review of the previous day's story.
- After reading the story, include Short Passage Practice on a daily basis.

Extended Units: If several children begin to score No Passes or barely pass, extend the unit by adding decoding and fluency practice. For 2 or 3 days, reteach an exercise page and use a homework passage for fluency practice.

Jell-Well Reviews: A Jell-Well Review is the *Read Well* term for a review of earlier units. A Jell-Well Review is a period of time taken to celebrate what children have learned and an opportunity to firm up their foundation of learning. To complete a Jell-Well Review, take the group back to the last unit for which all students scored Strong Passes. Then quickly cycle back up. See the *Assessment Manual* for how to build a Jell-Well Review.

Added Practice Options for Individual Students

Tutorials: Set up five-minute tutorials on a daily basis with an assistant, trained volunteer, or cross-age tutor. Have the tutor provide Short Passage Practice and Timed Readings.

Double Dose: Find ways to provide a double dose of *Read Well* instruction.
• Have the student work in his or her group *and* a lower-performing group.
• Have an instructional assistant, older student, or parent volunteer preview or review lessons.
• Preview new lessons or review previous lessons.

END-OF-THE-UNIT CELEBRATION

When students pass the Oral Reading Fluency Assessment, celebrate with the Certificate of Achievement on page 122.

Note: Using the Flesch-Kincaid Grade Level readability formula, the Unit 20 Assessment has a 3.1 readability level. Readabilities are based on number of words per sentence and number of syllables per word. Adding one or two multisyllabic words can increase readability by a month or two. Though we are attending to readability for the assessments, the overriding factor is decodability.

Wonderful Work

Andrew

has successfully completed

Read Well 2 Unit 20 • The Magic School Bus: Inside the Human Body

with 120 words correct per minute.

Teacher Signature *Mrs. Smith*

Date *March 3*

TRICKY WORD and FOCUS SKILL WARM-UP

stomach	microscope	gurgling	disgusting	unbelievable	examine

ORAL READING FLUENCY PASSAGE

The Best Day of My Life

⭐Some day I'm going to be a doctor. For me, science   11
class is always exciting. Last week we studied the human body.   22
Our teacher had us learn about the stomach first. We watched   33
a film and heard a gurgling stomach. We saw chunks of food   45
that the stomach was churning and mashing around. It looked   55
disgusting and very cool!   59

Next, we looked at giant red blood cells under a   69
microscope. The cells jumped and bounced around like big red   79
balls. Our teacher said that blood cells go on a wild ride through 92
the heart, lungs, and brain.   97

The most unbelievable thing happened last Friday. A   105
doctor came to our class and brought a real pig's heart for us   118
to examine. It was fascinating. Someone told me later that the   129
whole class turned green. Everyone but me. I got to hold the   141
heart, but nobody else did. That was the best day of my life!   154

ORAL READING FLUENCY	Start timing at the ⭐. Mark errors. Make a single slash in the text (/) at 60 seconds. If the student completes the passage in less than 60 seconds, have the student go back to the ⭐ and continue reading. Make a double slash (//) in the text at 60 seconds.
WCPM	Determine words correct per minute by subtracting errors from words read in 60 seconds.
STRONG PASS	The student scores no more than 2 errors on the first pass through the passage and reads 123 or more words correct per minute. Proceed to Unit 21.
PASS	The student scores no more than 2 errors on the first pass through the passage and reads 102 to 122 words correct per minute. Proceed to Unit 21.
NO PASS	The student scores 3 or more errors on the first pass through the passage and/or reads 101 or fewer words correct per minute. Provide added decoding and fluency practice. For 2 or 3 days, reteach an exercise page and use a homework passage for fluency practice, then retest.

Wonderful Work

_____

has successfully completed

Read Well 2 Unit 20 • *The Magic School Bus: Inside the Human Body*

with _____ words correct per minute.

Teacher Signature _____

Date _____

✂ -

Wonderful Work

_____

has successfully completed

Read Well 2 Unit 20 • *The Magic School Bus: Inside the Human Body*

with _____ words correct per minute.

Teacher Signature _____

Date _____